The Left Hand of Eden

The Left Hand of Eden

MEDITATIONS ON NATURE AND HUMAN NATURE

William Ashworth

Oregon State University Press
Corvallis

The paper in this book meets the guidelines for permanence and durability of the Committee on Production Guidelines for Book Longevity of the Council on Library Resources and the minimum requirements of the American National Standard for Permanence of Paper for Printed Library Materials Z39.48-1984.

Library of Congress Cataloging-in-Publication Data
Ashworth, William, 1942 -
The left hand of Eden : meditations on nature and human nature / William Ashworth
   p. cm.
Includes bibliographical references
ISBN 0-87071-460-0 (alk. paper)
1. Human ecology. 2. Philosophy of nature. I. Title.
GF21 .A84 1999
304.2—dc21

                            98-54935
                                 CIP

Oregon State University Press
101 Waldo Hall
Corvallis OR 97331-6407
541-737-3166 •fax 541-737-3170
http://.osu.orst.edu/dept/press

This time it's for Tom.

Everything exists, everything is true, and the earth is only a little dust under our feet.
                    —William Butler Yeats, *The Celtic Twilight*

We read that the traveller asked the boy if the swamp before him had a hard bottom. The boy replied that it had. But presently the traveller's horse sank in up to the girths, and he observed to the boy, "I thought you said that this bog had a hard bottom." "So it has," answered the latter, "but you have not got half way to it yet."
                    —Henry David Thoreau, *Walden*

Table of Contents

Prologue

This book is about the disharmony that exists between the laws of nature and the laws we use to protect it. It is about unity with nature, but with a twist: rather than bemoaning the lack of this unity in our lives, it points to the problems caused by our failure to recognize that it is there all the time. We are all of us, always, subject to natural law. We can manipulate its results, but we cannot change its operation; we may be able to mask its effects on us for a while, but we will never be able to eliminate them.

As a society, we are in deep denial about this. The development community and the preservation movement share alike in this denial. Both assume that the laws of nature are somehow modified or suspended within the areas we have developed, and are fully released only in the areas we have preserved. One side wishes to release more; the other side wishes to suspend or to modify more. That is the extent of their disagreement.

Both civilization and preservation, however, are human inventions. The borders we draw between them are human borders, totally unrecognized by nature. As a result, neither civilization nor preservation act in the manner that we think (hope; wish; demand) they should. All things on the planet are subject to the laws of nature first and the laws of humans second. Where the two come into conflict, it is always nature that prevails.

This is not the myth we grew up with. We were taught to think of nature as Other: tame versus wild, city versus country, farm versus forest, woodlot versus wilderness. Some have seen in that dichotomy an excuse for civilizing—for cutting, for converting, for removing raw materials for "beneficial use." Others have preferred preservation: a lockup, a line in the sand, a place apart where the Other may live unbounded and unkempt. Neither side has seen the truth: that nature can be neither civilized nor preserved. That "nature," as they conceive of it, does not in fact exist. Only the universe exists, and we as part of it, affecting everything we touch and either flourishing or withering by the result—as does all life.

The word "nature" comes down to us from the Latin *natura*. It was derived from *natus*, "birth," and in its original usage it simply meant physical kinship—the innate characteristics and traits shared among family members as a result of their common genetic heritage. We use this sense of the word today when we refer to "human nature" or to "the nature of things." But *natura* was also used in Latin to differentiate the natural world—the "world of born"—from the manufactured world—the "world of made"—and it is the twist we have given to this alternative meaning that has got us into trouble. For the Romans, the second meaning was a logical extension of the first, a means to distinguish the innate characteristics and traits of the world from the uses to which we have put them. For us, it has become a separation between two radically different types of reality, the works of God on the one hand and the works of technology on the other. We look at our cities and our automobiles and our computers and our TV dinners and think we have created something. We have not. All we have done is use pre-created rules to put pre-created things together in new ways.

This book is couched as a collection of nature essays, and because of the subject matter it has been necessary to use the "n-word" many times. I have tried to hew close to the meaning as understood by the Romans: nature as the heritage we start with, rather than as the ideal we worship or the enemy we conquer and then banish. "Nature," in these pages, may mean a set of shared, inherited characteristics—human nature, bear nature, the world's nature—or it may mean the world of born, the pieces of the planet (any pieces, perhaps as small as weeds that have anchored themselves in cracks in a sidewalk) that we humans have not yet significantly manipulated. Sometimes it will mean the set of rules through which the universe operates. Only rarely will it mean something apart from us, and only then to discount that faulty and dangerous idea. The Otherness of nature is a myth that has controlled our lives long enough. It is time to put it aside, as any ancient and outworn mythology is put aside, and move along.

The essays that make up this book were written over a period of approximately one and one-half years, from November 1994 through March 1996. Although they were conceived as a unit, they are independent in content, and may be read individually. They are organized here into three broad sections.

The three essays in the first section ("The Undiscovered Journey") deal with the changelessness of change. Natural law does not alter, but it operates by altering everything it touches. Life is continuous, though individuals die; geology is constant, though landscapes shift. The world is timeless, but every moment is new.

The six essays that make up the second section ("The Enemy of Progress") describe some of the workings of natural law as they apply throughout both the world of born and the world of made. Human structures and human time scales do not constrain nature, which operates chaotically—a term now understood as being not without rules or logic, but without linearity. The universe is comprehensively synergistic: no whole can be explained by summing its parts. Emotions are not a human invention, but are one of the chief driving forces of the living world. The flow of time requires both beginnings and endings, which for living things means both birth and death, both speciation and extinction. And the planet's edges are fuzzy. There are no clean-cut boundaries here; there are only limits, which life—optimistic by nature (there is that word again!)—always tries to exceed.

The third and final section, "The Left Hand of Eden," attempts a synthesis. Its four essays are built around a common theme: that all attempts to separate the world of born from the world of made are fundamentally flawed, and thus doomed. This caution applies alike to those who would conquer nature and to those who would preserve it. The lock-it-all-up mentality is as faulty as the cut-it-all-down mentality; preservation destroys integration with the biosphere as thoroughly as clearcutting does. Nature—the old, robust Roman *natura*—is everywhere. You cannot compartmentalize it. All you can do is compartmentalize yourself.

Some who have reviewed this work have pointed to the fact that it presents many problems, but few solutions. To this I plead guilty. I have always been a little suspicious of the pat "solutions" offered at the end of most books about society's problems; they usually seem a little too good to be true, and on close examination they almost always prove to be exactly that. So I have avoided preaching about The Way Things Ought To Be, and limited myself to describing the way things actually are.

To those who insist on formalizing solutions, however, I would say this: do not look for them in prescriptions and proscriptions on human behavior. That ground has been tilled and found sterile. Seek instead for means to promote understanding, and for methods to encourage and enable a proper respect for our role as natural participants. We cannot elevate nature over the human appetite for progress, because this appetite is itself natural, a direct result of the ancient quest of our DNA for its own longevity and security. However, we can do the next best thing: we can redefine "progress." Work on that redefinition.

"Conservation," wrote that old conservationist, Gifford Pinchot, many years ago, "is the application of common sense to the common problems for the common good." Though we may quibble over the meanings of the terms involved, the definition itself is sound. If we are going to make any headway against the environmental problems that vex us, I think we are going to have to resurrect Pinchot. Ever since he broke with John Muir over Hetch Hetchy he has been branded a traitor. We must get over these petty vendettas. Though Pinchot certainly made errors—Hetch Hetchy was one of them—the basic thrust of his work was correct. Careful use of resources is the key to preserving them. It not only works: it is the only thing that ever has.

May these essays be modest steps in that direction.

William Ashworth
Ashland, Oregon
February 24, 1998

I. The Undiscovered Journey

A Death at Sunset

The beach at the mouth of Brushy Creek focused the westering sun like a parabolic glass. To the south loomed the immense black bulk of Humbug Mountain; to the north, the tawny, truncated hills of Coal Point dropped like a golden balustrade into the sea. The breakers of the Pacific, backlit, kept up their ancient, tireless beat of thrust and withdrawal, the silvered rift tendriling up the beach and sinking, mirrored, into the sand. The light was golden; the waves were translucent green. Small knots of people sat on the sand or wandered slowly along the edge of the surf, looking westward. And there was the dying seal.

The seal lay at the back of the beach, where the storms of many winters had cross-sectioned an ancient landslide, leaving stones, sticks, and whole trees exposed in a thirty-foot cutbank. Tucked into the base of a steep gully in that sandy wall, the color of sand itself, the seal did not immediately attract notice: my wife and I, intent on the September sunset, were well past before another couple called it to our attention. It lay half on its side, its flanks heaving with the effort of breath, oblivious of us until we came to within about twenty feet. Then some small sound from feet or clothing made it lift its head. Black eyes, with plenty of self-awareness still in them, locked onto mine. There was a soundless gape of defiance, but the animal was clearly too weak to do anything more.

There rises within most of us at such times a deep, almost desperate urge to *do* something. The suffering of other creatures brings out the altruist in us: we want to ease the pain, prevent the death, make things somehow whole and *right* again. Could we help the seal back into the sea? Had its plight been reported to the authorities at the Oregon state park on whose grounds it was sinking rapidly toward death? Had wildlife officials been consulted? Had a vet been called? We caught up with the couple who had first pointed the dying animal out to us, and my wife, with her characteristic gift for directness, managed to roll all of these questions into one. *Do you know*, she asked, *how long it has been like this?*

They knew. The seal had first come ashore, they said, four days previously. In the beginning it had moved about a bit, and even earlier this day they had noticed it throwing sand on itself with its flippers, evidently in an attempt to keep cool, though it didn't look up to doing even that any more. Park authorities and wildlife officials seemed unconcerned. Seals pulling themselves ashore to die are not a new phenomenon. There was nothing they—or we—could do.

That night I lay in my sleeping bag in the park campground, my ears tuned to the ripple of Brushy Creek and the distant, faint boom of the Pacific surf, and thought of the dying animal a half mile away. What was it about the death of a seal that should bother me so? Death is a necessary part of life; it is nature's way of making certain the earth doesn't fill up. It provides a constant small trickle of open spaces in each ecological niche, thus driving evolution and speciation and creating the fascinating variety of living things on this planet. The death of other organisms keeps us alive; this is true whether you are a hunter wolfing down a slab of venison or a vegetarian who merely wolfs down lettuce and celery and apples. Plants, after all, are also living things. Lettuce and celery are killed by the harvest, and though you may comfort yourself with the thought that the apple tree, at least, remains alive, the apple itself is a separate entity that continues to metabolize right up to the time you bite into it. Death is natural, the inevitable result of natural law. Why do we humans spend so much time and energy keeping it at bay, not only for ourselves but for others—even when, as in this case, "other" means not only a different individual but a different species?

The reason, of course, is that while death may be necessary and good for life as a whole, and even for the species whose members die, it is bad for the individual who is dying. Death is a terminus; beyond lies nothing we can know, except through speculation and faith. We therefore resist termination. Because we are a social species, dependent on each other for survival, we resist the termination of other members of our society as well. And because we are a preeminently empathetic species—a characteristic born of the marriage of our social-animal altruism with our oversized brains—we find it easy to expand the definition of "our" society to include all creatures with sufficient self-awareness that we can believe they might suffer. Most of us will pull weeds or slap mosquitoes with no sense of disturbance, but we will spend thousands of dollars to preserve the life of a favorite dog or cat. This is only partly for the benefit of the dog or the cat. By preventing an animal's death, we also prevent our own pain at having to watch the death, as well as eliminating an uncomfortable reminder of our own mortality. It is as much our suffering as the animal's that we are concerned about.

A few years before my encounter with the dying seal, in the course of research for a book on bears, I had interviewed Dave Siddon, formerly a cinematographer for the Walt

Disney organization, who was then—until his death from cancer too short a time later—the director of a large wildlife rehabilitation center near Grants Pass, Oregon. Siddon had been very blunt on this point. "Everyone says what a wonderful service we provide for wildlife," he told me. "But we're not providing a service for wildlife—we're providing a service for people who *care* about wildlife. We provide a human service for people who care enough to bring animals to us. We think they need to be encouraged to continue to care. The fact is, if we look on *Homo sapiens* as the only life form worth saving, it probably isn't."

Siddon's brutal honesty about his calling can be applied with equal validity to other fields of environmental endeavor besides wildlife rehabilitation. In truth, *all* environmental protection is at heart human protection. It is really us that we want to save—us, and our world as we want it to be, complete with wild places and spectacular scenery and clean air. Environmental protection began with the superlatives—with the Yellowstones and Yosemites and Grand Canyons—because we wanted them to still be there if we ever got a chance to see them. It proceeded to natural places in general because we prefer natural places to (for instance) downtown Los Angeles and we want to make sure there will always be enough to go around. It encompasses clean air and clean water because they are healthier and more pleasant for humans to consume. And it embraces endangered-species protection—and the protection of wildlife in general, including dying seals on a beach—because, as a species and particularly as a culture, we are uncomfortable to the point of irrationality with the idea and experience of death, and find it emotionally necessary to keep the Reaper at bay as long as possible.

None of this is meant to belittle the environmental movement or the people who give their lives to it. We need, as Siddon said, to continue to care. Protecting wildlands, saving endangered species, and increasing the health of the environment are right and proper, and it is necessary to keep doing these things. But we ought to understand why we do them. It is not to protect life on the planet—life will survive, anyway. A force that can arise in the extraordinarily hostile conditions on a newborn planet, and can thrive equally well today in the screaming ice storms of an Antarctic winter and in the hot, sulfurous, lightless waters of thermal vents on the deep ocean floor, is going to be able to endure pretty much anything we can throw at it. Life will survive. It is the human race that is in doubt.

Because our species has been so successful at manipulating natural forces to our own ends, we have somehow got the idea that we now stand outside these forces and so control them. This is pernicious nonsense. We have never eradicated a single law of nature nor escaped its consequences. We have played them off against each other, using the results of some to counter the results of others, and have managed to gain some benefit from them through this process; but we have not "harnessed" them, and we have certainly not separated ourselves from them. We may heat our homes and generate electricity through combustion, but we must also live with the other results of the laws that allow combustion to happen, including muddled views, respiratory disease, and acid rain. Aerodynamics may give the appearance of conquering gravity, but gravity still operates, and when aerodynamic lift is reduced too far a plane still falls to the ground.

What is true for the laws of combustion and aerodynamics holds as well for the rest of the laws of nature. The principles governing population dynamics, climate, landform development, energy flow through ecosystems, growth, and ecological succession are as immutable as the principles that send electrons down wires, or produce tightly controlled explosions to propel vehicles down highways, or guide the combination of atoms into molecules and of girders into buildings. We can manipulate the results of these laws, but we cannot change the laws themselves. Relaxation of environmental resistance still leads to overpopulation, whether it is cattle protected from predators or predators protected from hunters. Overpopulation still leads to resource degradation, whether it is deer in a crowded forest, livestock on an overgrazed range, or humans on a small, blue planet spinning around a medium-sized, class-G star. Shore drift still moves sand along coastlines. Sunlight still drives photosynthesis. Earthquakes still build mountains. Winds still blow.

And things still die. On a beach at sunset; in a hospital bed, harnessed to feeding tubes and monitors; in the heart of a forest, with chainsaws tearing through bark into the living cambium layer beneath; in the garden, snatched from the nurturing safety of the soil to be cut into chunks and dropped into stewpots. Flies die bumbling against windowpanes; petunias die with the frost, after one bright, brief season in the sun. Death is our constant companion. Year after year, the Centers for Disease Control in Atlanta releases statistics on the prime causes of death among Americans. Year after year it is wrong. The leading cause of death is not cancer or heart disease or AIDS; the leading cause of death is life. It may take more than a century, but birth is always one hundred percent fatal.

Instinctively, we deny this. Driven by the ancient urge of our chromosomes to preserve and replicate themselves, we crave immortality, not only for ourselves, but also for the things we love. For wild things—the damp, rich smell of forests in the rain, the wind across the tundra, the rustle of rivers in the darkness, the surge of birds through the autumn air. For pleasurable things—good food and good wine, a fire on a winter's night, conversations with friends, tales woven skillfully by authors or acted movingly on the stage or screen. For familiar things—our own homes, our own jobs, our own families; the grove of trees we have known since childhood; old prices, old tax levels, old rules. And for dreams and the right to chase them—the mother lode, the winning lottery ticket, the resources to build an empire. Wealth for all citizens. Peace among all nations. Liberty. Justice. Love.

There is nothing wrong with any of these things, except for this: not one of them is permanent. Heraclitus had it right. All things are in motion, nothing is at rest. You cannot step into the same river twice. The only unchanging thing in the universe is change itself. Attempts to preserve anything—jobs, or private property rights, or forests, or clean water, or economic growth, or equal opportunity—will always run up against the incontrovertible, uncomfortable, fundamental presence of impermanence. Every religion has an afterlife, because none of us can conceive of ourselves as not existing. But change is inescapable. And so is death.

Outside the tent there was a brief scratching and rustling, as some small animal attempted to open the bag of potato chips we had left on the campsite table. Beside me my wife stirred. In the distance the surf kept up its restless, heavy serenade to the dying seal. Lives ticking past; change occurring; deaths approaching, my own death among them. An oddly comforting thought. All of us are one with the rest of the natural world after all, at death if at no time else. Air ebbs and flows through lungs or leaves; blood pumps, sap rises and falls; the Krebs cycle churns, and churns, and eventually runs down. Old organisms die. New organisms, new species and genera, whole new kingdoms of living things arise to take their place. Science calls it "punctuated continuity." It is life.

Witnesses to the Creation

On the outer flank of Cape Cod, facing the gray Atlantic, a long line of pale bluffs stands like a bulwark against a threat anticipated for so many centuries that even the identity of the enemy has been forgotten. Just past the south end of this rim of ruined keeps, on a dune near the outer tip of the narrow spit that shelters the northern part of Nauset Marsh from the sea, a Boston gentleman named Henry Beston had a small house built. This was in 1925. The house was intended only as a weekend retreat, so its design was kept Spartan. Two rooms, one for the bed and the other for everything else. A fireplace between the rooms for heat; a pipe driven straight down into the dune for water. What its owner termed "a somewhat amateur enthusiasm" of windows—ten in all, three in the smaller room and six in the larger plus a small, rectangular "look-see" in the only door. Beston called the place the Fo'c'sle.

Henry Beston Sheahan was thirty-seven years old, a tall, dapper, French-Irish American with a taste for natty clothes and concertina music who was trying to make it as a writer. He was a good amateur naturalist, but had not yet thought to write about nature. In 1919 he had published a book about his experiences during the Great War as a member of the fledgling U.S. Navy Submarine Corps; it was called *Full Speed Ahead*, but it was actually pretty much dead in the water. Since then he had written mostly children's books. His romance with the poet Elizabeth Coatsworth seemed as stalled as his career. In early September, 1926, driven by a need to get away from Boston for a while, he went down to the Fo'c'sle to begin what was projected as a two-week stay. "The fortnight ending," he wrote later, "I lingered on, and as the year lengthened into autumn, the beauty and mystery of this earth and outer sea so possessed and held me that I could not go." The roles had been reversed; the cape had become his home, the city his weekend retreat. Except for brief visits, it would be a full year before he returned to Boston.

The journal of that year on the sand, lovingly polished and honed, was published in the fall of 1928 as *The Outermost House*. There are many—I am among them— who consider this taut, elemental, beautifully crafted work the finest piece of nature writing America has yet produced.

On August 31, 1992—as chance would have it, 65 years to the day from the "night so luminous and still" on which Beston, sleeping outside under the stars, came to the reluctant conclusion that it was time for his solitary experiment to end—my wife and I drove to the Doane Rock picnic area by Nauset Marsh, left the car, and took the marsh trail eastward toward Coast Guard Beach and the sea. It was late afternoon. "There are nights in summer when darkness and ebbing tide quiet the universal wind," wrote Beston, "and this August night was full of that quiet of absence, and the sky was clear." This August night was like that, too. The marsh side of the dune line was golden, the ocean side gray with shadow. On the great beach, "solitary and elemental, unsullied and remote, visited and possessed by the outer sea," only a few other strollers lingered. We headed south.

Cape Cod is moving. A great clot of morainal clays and gravels shed by the Pleistocene ice sheet just before it began retreating north, it is heaped loosely on the shallow continental shelf. Constant worrying by the immense dog of the sea shakes bits and pieces loose from the pile; these are picked up by currents and moved off, to be redeposited anywhere from a few inches to a few miles away. In this manner the whole cape migrates shoreward, changing shape as it goes. The migration is faster than we think. In the middle of the nineteenth century, when men sought whales with wooden ships and hand-thrown harpoons, whalers gathered to exchange news and await incoming ships on a large island near Wellfleet, next to the cape's inner shore. That piece of land is still called Great Island, but it is now a peninsula. The moving cape overtook it years ago: the Herring River, which once entered Cape Cod Bay through an opening north of the island known as The Gut, now empties into Wellfleet Harbor.

Further evidence of the dynamic nature of this landscape can be found on the outer beaches. Walking south in the waning light, we stumbled regularly upon outcroppings of a dark, crumbly material, clearly organic in origin, low on the beach at the edge of the breakers where it was constantly shredded by wave action and the beaks of shorebirds. This dark evanescence is peat, formed on the floor of the marsh sheltered behind Nauset Spit when the spit was at least a half mile further to the east. The spit has climbed right over it, and now sits on a floor of peat. How far this motion has progressed over the centuries is anyone's guess; peat is soft stuff and disappears swiftly when exposed, leaving no evidence behind. But some parts of the nearby bluffs, we know, are eroding backward as rapidly as two to three feet a year. If the rate here is even a foot a year, the eleven centuries since the withdrawal of the ice would have seen Nauset Spit shift more than two miles toward Rhode Island. If the rate is two feet a year, the beach that Henry Beston walked was more than 100 feet seaward of the waves now crashing at our wandering feet.

The Earth is alive. I do not mean this in a Lovelockian, organic, neo-Gaian sense—though I would not want to rule that out entirely - but in the less mystical sense of a physical structure constantly evolving and changing, recreating itself continuously according to an ancient set of rules we are only just now beginning to vaguely understand. The continents drift back and forth, the oceans contract and expand; ice huddles at the poles and makes periodic forays outward as far as halfway to the equator. Mountains thrust upward and are carried, grain by microscopic grain, back to the encompassing sea. The sea itself shifts. Currents swirl through it; water comes constantly into it from the mouths of rivers and leaves constantly from it, climbing ladders of sunlight to the clouds, which drift over the land to create the rivers. The winds that carry the clouds also shift, and with them the rainfall, and with the rainfall the vegetation. Cape Cod, when it was born, was naked. Oak and beech, maple and pine, barberry and cranberry and saltgrass—all these are arrivals not much older than the fields and lawns and gardens now grown almost universally on the cape in their stead. Geology is not only about the past. Geology is also the here and now.

If we had any doubts, Mt. St. Helens should have silenced them. The blast that tore through that picturesque Washington State volcano in the early hours of May 18, 1980, scattered pieces of its cone as far away as Kansas. Roads in eastern Washington, 100 miles away, were obliterated under falling ash. Whole forests were felled; the shapes of lakes and rivers were changed. Near the small town of Castle Rock, beside Interstate 5 and a mile or so south of the junction of the Toutle and Cowlitz rivers, there is today a large, flat-topped, curiously regular hill, covered with grass and busily becoming part of the scenery. It began life as a dump. A huge quantity of Mt. St. Helens was washing down the Toutle in the aftermath of the explosion, and the frantic engineers cleaning it out of the Cowlitz and the nearby Columbia piled most of it up at Castle Rock simply to get it out of the way. It is still there, and looks a safe bet to survive about as long as the mountain itself.

In March, 1963—the spring of my sophomore year in college—I climbed Mt. St. Helens with two classmates as equally ill-prepared and adventure-hungry as I. We left Portland at midnight and began hiking south from Spirit Lake, under a full moon, at about 2:00 a.m. The road to Timberline Cabin lay deep beneath snow, and we moved heavily in our snowshoes. We reached the buried cabin at the same time as the sun did, a little after 6:00. The mountain loomed over us, elemental and arctic. A pause for breakfast and to exchange our snowshoes for crampons, then it was onward and upward, over Dog's Head and up the eastern limb of the Forsythe Glacier to the summit. The greatest danger faced by climbers on St. Helens in those days was disorientation. "The smooth symmetry of the peak makes route-finding problems great, especially when fog covers the mountain," warned the American Alpine Club in the 1960 edition of its *Climber's Guide to the Cascade and Olympic Mountains of Washington*, "and it is easy to descend the wrong side of the peak."

No more. St. Helens today is a ragged, hollowed-out stump of a peak, a broken tooth looking for a root canal. Aircraft fly through the precise spot where I once stood shivering on the summit, nearly a third of a vertical mile above what is now the nearest ground. Dog's Head and Timberline Cabin and the Forsythe Glacier have evaporated as thoroughly as the snows that once covered them. As thoroughly as the beach that Henry Beston walked, or the beach of the proto-Cape Cod, washed by the now featureless Atlantic far to the darkening east.

When we speak of these, and similar, processes—earthquakes, floods, wildfires, hurricanes—it is common to use the language of destruction: the mountain is blown up, the beach is washed away, forests are wiped out by fire or storm, the earth is broken by fault lines. Even professionals get caught up in this. Here is geologist Robert D. Ballard, writing about Mt. St. Helens for *National Geographic*:

> *Shaken by a 5.0-magnitude earthquake deep in its bowels, Mount St. Helens tore 390 m off its crown and spewed a cloud of smoke and ash 21 km into the stratosphere. Out of its north flank roared a holocaust of hot debris and scalding gases at 320 kmph (200 mph), triggering devastating mudflows and floods, and claiming the lives of 64 people.*

Small wonder that the landscape north of St. Helens—in company with the similar but somewhat smaller area to the east of Lassen Peak in California that was affected by that mountain's 1916 eruption—is now identified on maps as the Devastated Area.

But is this entirely fair? These landscape-altering events have at least as much to do with renewal as they do with destruction. St. Helens may indeed be, as geologists Charles Plummer and David McGeary have termed it, a "darkened, gouged-out stump," but that stump is as right and proper as the pure symmetry that preceded it. It is not as smooth, but it is more interesting. Lands are born this way. Landscape is a promise that is rewritten even as it is being continuously kept. Like the clouds that mimic them, the mountains shift. The grains of stone that the wind scours from the

Matterhorn are displaced as thoroughly as the summit of St. Helens, and given enough time they will add up to as much. The Cape Cod that will greet tomorrow's sun is, in the strictest sense of the word, a new earth under a new heaven. *Terra* is only *firma* in the limited vision of the human race.

The vanished glaciers that gave the first shape to these outermost sands also marked much of the rest of the continent. The Great Lakes were formed by ice; so were the canyons of Yosemite and the peaks of the Rockies. In Nebraska, a vast, cold Sahara of glacial drift was blown about by the winds until grasses stabilized it and, over time, its dunes became the Sand Hills. In Montana, a lake the size of Erie backed up behind an ice dam in Cabinet Gorge, just west of what is now the Idaho border; the flood that was released when the ice failed scoured most of the soil off the Channeled Scablands of eastern Washington and carried house-sized pieces of the Montana mountains as far west as the Willamette Valley of western Oregon.

Because they are revealed to us primarily through the geologic record, there is a tendency to dismiss these events as things of the ancient past, a restlessness of the young planet that is no longer relevant today. In truth, most of the shaping events of these northern landscapes had human witnesses, and some postdate the invention of writing. When the Missoula Flood swept most of eastern Washington down the Columbia to the sea, people were there. When Minnesota, North Dakota, and Manitoba rose slowly from the waves of the now-vanished Lake Agassiz, people were there. When Crater Lake was born from the ragged womb of Mt. Mazama, following an explosive eruption forceful enough to make Mt. St. Helens look like popped bubble gum, Ur of the Chaldees had been settled and science had started in Egypt. When Lakes Superior, Huron, and

Michigan were formed by the downcutting of the St. Clair River and the partial draining of Glacial Lake Nipigon, the pyramids had been ruins for more than 2000 years.

Given the dance of the earth's surface through geologic time there is no reason to believe that it should stop now, and indeed it has not. James Hutton, the eighteenth-century Edinburgh physician whose *Theory of the Earth* underlies and anticipates most of the modern science of geology, continues to have the last laugh at his critics. "The present," wrote Hutton, "is the key to the past." Geologic forces remain uniform through time. The results of those forces may appear in fits and starts—Mt. St. Helens is proof enough of that—but the forces themselves, all of them, are observable today, and are no less active now than they were in the Pleistocene epoch, or indeed the Precambrian era, when the first bacteria were forming in the first seas under a sun that was still new and young.

From his window in Portland, Oregon, scientist and Quaker elder Ellis Jump observed the drama of the St. Helens eruption and knew that the awe he felt had nothing to do with destruction. "We are witnesses to the Creation," he noticed himself proclaiming. "God has not stopped making the world. He continues to keep His covenant." Jump was correct, but incomplete; in truth, we are all witnesses to the Creation. The finger of God's hand still strokes the universe, disguised as geology. We do not often feel the finger's touch, but it is there constantly. All lands are impermanent; every inch of the planetary surface is always undergoing change. Rock is a river, flowing more slowly than water, but just as surely, carrying the continents, molecule by molecule and age by age, into the waiting cradle of the sea. You do not need a Mt. St. Helens, or even a Cape Cod, to show you this. Plant a tree and watch it grow; mow your lawn, water it, and mow it again. Visit any slope in the rain. The amount displaced downhill by each drop is infinitesimally small, but there are many drops and they have all of time in which to work. Ponder the words of Isaiah. It may take longer than he thought, but the geology of this passage is perfectly sound:

> *Every valley shall be exalted, and every mountain*
> *and hill shall be made low: and the crooked shall be*
> *made straight, and the rough places plain.*

Love impermanence. Love it, not simply because you cannot escape it; love it because, without the continuous gift of renewal that it brings, life on earth would not be possible. Love it because you are a part of it. Your birth and mine were new and singular events. If the world had been complete the day it was brought into being, then no one alive today could have ever possibly been born.

We had reached the end of the beach. A few feet beyond us, Nauset Spit stopped and Nauset Inlet began. A quarter mile away the sand took up again, a spit the mirror of this one, starting at the inlet and stretching south; but that was another world, the far side of the looking-glass, where we could never go without a white rabbit in a waistcoat to lead us. Or at least a long trip by foot and automobile. Nauset Marsh and Nauset Bay were in shadow; in the whole of the visible world, only the tops of the nearby dunes still caught the sun. This too would soon pass. Saltgrass blades cast shade far bigger than themselves, one last puff of self-importance before the obscurity of night. A semipalmated plover marched up a nearby dune, dragging an ostrich-sized shadow, working the rapidly waning sunsurf as its brothers on the beach worked the white rift of the darkening sea.

Nauset Inlet was a river flowing toward the Atlantic. Cape Cod is in what is termed a mesotidal region, meaning that the tidal rise and fall is moderate to large; the inlet here is small relative to the size of the bay and the marsh behind it, and when the ocean draws down in obedience to the moon the water level in the bay takes some time to adjust. During that time the current outward is intense. When the sea rises again, it meets and overtakes the falling bay; then the current reverses, and the flow is inward. Grains of sand at the tip of the spit move out with the ebb of the tide, in with its flow; at the point of balance between ebb and flow the longshore current takes over, and the sand moves south. Thus the inlet advances to the north. This advance is considerably faster than the advance of the cape itself toward the North American mainland. At the Salt Pond Visitor Center in Eastham, a Park Service ranger had handed me a map and warned me not to trust it. "The inlet is in the wrong place on this," she said. "They can't keep up with it in the map department." And she marked a line on the map to show the approximate location of the current inlet, a good half-mile north of the one the cartographers had drawn. Now at that line's locus, we climbed the southernmost dune and, from its summit, gazed about us at the great marsh and the great beach and the night coming out of the east over the dark, stirring mystery of the sea.

On October 11, 1964, Henry Beston came to this open world of beach and sky for what turned out to be the last time. The Fo'c'sle was being dedicated as a National Literary Landmark, and the dunes were full of Important People. There were speeches. Beston sat through them, wrapped in a coat and his memories. He said little. The house was no longer his: he had donated it to the Massachusetts Audubon Society four years previously for use as a weekend retreat, and now the speakers were claiming it for an even larger society, a part of the cultural heritage of all America. It was also no longer on its original site. In a moving landscape of sand and sea a building site has to have a certain amount of give to it. Beston had been forced to move the building once himself, and the Audubon Society was already preparing to move it again. The speakers wound down; a permanent brass plaque was attached to a corner of the impermanent structure. Beston went home to Maine, to the farm near Nobleboro which he and Elizabeth Coatsworth had purchased shortly after their marriage in 1930. On April 15, 1968, he died there, a few miles inland from the rocky shores of Muscongus Bay—a scoured and polished world that was in all probability the source of much of the material the glacier had carried south to form what had become Cape Cod.

The Outermost House lived less than ten years longer. On February 6, 1978, a great storm came out of the North Atlantic to batter Nauset Spit and its backbone of dunes. When the storm withdrew the house was gone. The dedicatory plaque came riding in on a wave and was deposited on the beach near the skewed but still intact outhouse. The inlet had moved closer; it was increasingly clear that it would soon claim the site of the Fo'c'sle itself.

What does one do with a literary landmark when there is no longer any land to mark? One leaves it mercifully to the wind and sea. Standing on this dune, facing south, I gazed at a spot in the air. On that spot, as insubstantial as the vanished summit of St. Helens that my own booted feet had once trod, Beston had spent his outermost year. A gull swept through, screaming. Directly below it, in the inlet, the trapped waters of the Atlantic raced outward toward freedom. I felt, once again, the exultation that comes from witnessing the ongoing birth of the planet.

Beston would have understood that exultation. I know this because he said so. Here is the passage as it appears, italics and all, almost at the end of *The Outermost House*:

> *During the months that have passed since that*
> *September morning some have asked me what*
> *understanding of Nature one shapes from so strange*
> *a year? I would answer that one's first appreciation is*
> *a sense that the creation is still going on, that the*
> *creative forces are as great and as active to-day as*
> *they have ever been, and that to-morrow's morning*
> *will be as heroic as any of the world. Creation is here*
> *and now. So near is man to the creative pageant, so*
> *much a part is he of the endless and incredible*
> *experiment, that any glimpse he may have will be*
> *but the revelation of a moment, a solitary note heard*
> *in a symphony thundering through debatable*
> *existences of time. Poetry is as necessary to*
> *comprehension as science. It is as impossible to live*
> *without reverence as it is without joy.*

The scythe of time cuts soil and stone as easily as it cuts lives. Everything that moves has meaning, and everything moves. The things we build, the hands we build them with, the earth we build them on, are all transitory, and as with all things beautiful and temporary should be honored and beloved.

Does this mean there are no things permanent in the universe? It does not. *Process itself is permanent.* We are submersed continuously in the continuing miracle of Genesis. The most important human sense is the sense of wonder, for it is the only one that can begin to comprehend the fundamental nature of the world we have been given, and that fundamental nature is change, and it is the only miracle we need. The earth moves and the sea and sky change and the person you love breathes in and out, and it is all one phenomenon, here on the outer edge of the cape in the dying day or there at the foot of Mt. St. Helens on the morning of Creation or any time and any place in the loom and shuttle of the weaving world. Anywhere you are, there the earth lives.

The Undiscovered Journey

Once in Louisiana, beside a saltgrass-filled slough a few miles east of the Sabine River, I spent much of one long, late-summer afternoon observing an alligator. "Observing" may be a misleading term here, however, for it implies that I was seeing something. I was looking, but there was very little I could actually see. A dim, shadowy bulk beneath the water; a small bit of leathery forehead cleaving the surface; one bright eye intently observing me observing it. That was all. For most of the time that I sat there it lay still, a shape that might have been a log but for the alert gaze it carried. Once it crossed the slough, sliding imperceptibly into motion without so much as a ripple in the water, gliding perhaps fifteen feet, and halting by the near bank, again without appearing to disturb anything. There was, in fact, so little evidence of movement from either the animal or the water that it was almost easier to believe that they had stayed still and the banks of the slough had moved around them. It was possible to discern the point where the journey had begun, and where it had ended; it was impossible to make out the journey.

A few months before the alligator and I spent the afternoon eyeing each other, a startling news release had come from a pair of explorers encamped near the southern end of the Empty Quarter, that bone-dry, uninhabited waste of sand in southern Arabia through which runs the indeterminate boundary between Yemen and Oman. Here in the country where the Queen of Sheba once ruled, rumors of an immense trading center, half-legendary Ubar, City of Frankincense, had been surfacing periodically for generations. Now a pair of amateur archeologists—a documentary filmmaker and a Los Angeles lawyer—announced that they had found it. Analyzing photographs taken from the *Challenger* space shuttle, Nicholas Clapp and George Hedges had noticed something odd: numerous thin, spidery lines, nearly invisible at ground level but easily spotted from orbit, stretching for hundreds of miles through the deserted sands. They were the ghosts of vanished highways, marks made millennia ago by the passage of many camel caravans. The sand was ground more finely where the animals' hooves had crushed it, and this had caused a minute change in reflectivity that had shown up clearly only from space.

Tracing these barely physical pathways, Clapp and Hedges found a spot where most of them converged. On the day after Christmas, 1991, an expedition mounted by the two men began digging at the convergence, amid sand dunes as tall as forty-story buildings. They struck masonry almost immediately. Slowly from the dunes a ruined city emerged— house foundations, caravan encampments, and a magnificent, many-sided castle with at least nine towers anchoring its walls. A journey not taken for two thousand years had led at last to its ancient destination.

My own destination, one September Sunday not long ago, was the gravel bar along the Klamath River on which Dr. Gordon Enns had parked his Toyota station wagon. We were trying to find it from the river. Gordon is an M.D. from a small town in southern Oregon who spends most of his summer weekends drifting down bits of rivers on inflatable kayaks, the kind known generically by the trade name "Tahiti." This particular weekend my wife and I had joined him for a look at one of his favorites, a nine-mile run down the central part of the Klamath. Putting in at Tree of Heaven, a Forest Service campground and boat launch a few miles west of the Randolph Collier rest area on Interstate 5, we headed down-canyon, bobbing along on the back of the largest river in northern California. This was in no sense a wilderness experience—a two-lane paved highway, California 96, paralleled the river throughout the stretch we were running, and boat traffic, primarily other inflatables, was extremely high—but there was about it nevertheless a strong feeling of reconnection with the natural world. Birds perching on reeds and on the branches of willows serenaded our passage. The sky, bounded by the canyon walls, changed shape constantly. The river surged and muttered, thrusting us along. At intervals there were rapids; most of these were easy to run, though there was one stretch of Class III whitewater, Kanaka Falls, that required Gordon to talk the rest of us carefully through it. Being supported by the moving water, traveling at the pace and along the pathway that it determined, brought with it after a while a complete sense of integration with the river's life, creating a passage powerfully different from that along the shore—so different, in fact, that after we had finally located the right gravel bar, pulled out, and were headed back upstream in the Toyota with the deflated kayaks bobbing along in their trailer in our wake, I could locate almost no landmarks from the river journey, though nearly every foot of its course was easily visible from the highway.

All nature is in a continual state of becoming. Since the moment of the Big Bang roughly fifteen billion years ago the universe has been surging outward, expanding through the fabric of Creation, dragging space and time into being as it goes. We are carried on this surging current like infinitely small inflatables on an infinitely large river. The motion is powerful, but it is largely hidden. There are no visible disturbances in the current, no roadways, no easy points of congruence from one part of the journey to another. Only the alligator's eye; only the pattern made visible by distance. We travel the riverbank or the river, but never the two simultaneously. If there is a more urgent lesson than this, I do not know what it is.

On our small bit of tumbling mud, with stars and galaxies whirling dizzily around us and even the mud itself shifting beneath our feet, we live our lives as though the universe were static. It is perfectly understandable that we should live this way, but it is wrong. Stability is a comfortable delusion, but it is nonetheless a delusion. Whether we take note of it or not, the journey continues. Moment follows moment, age follows age; creatures and climates evolve, rivers wear through rock, the endless sea itself ends. A heartbeat ago in the life of the earth, woolly mammoths roamed the tundra along the margins of the ice that covered what is now Wisconsin. A heartbeat hence, who knows what strange lands and life forms there may be?

Always change.

Always change.

All ways change.

Outside my window the ground is drifted with plum leaves, variegated pink with slight blushes of orange and crimson. Further up the back yard the plum leaves give way to hawthorn, then to walnut, and finally to peach. Within the bodies of the trees, unseen, the sap has pulled back from the limbs as winter approaches. We have another six weeks of shortening days; then they will lengthen again. The waxwings that passed through in a chittering, billowing mass two weeks ago will pass through once more, headed north;

the juncos that come down to the valley with the winter will follow the spring upslope. I will be older. Looking back toward my birth I can begin to see the pathways in the sand. The river's bank passes by, or the river does; it all depends on your perspective, and it does not matter anyway. What matters is the reality of the passage.

The journey of Creation is continuous, and does not pause to accommodate the whims of the journeyers. The Guide did not walk away after six days. We travel together, dependent upon each other, and the rules of the road apply equally to us all. Look for the journey. Look for it in the fall of leaves and snow, the formation of soil, the bringing forth of buds and mountains. Examine your own breathing. Do not try to change these things. You are not stronger than Canute, nor wiser. It is necessary to be alert for certain signs: the right gravel bar, the right sand dune, the shape of the sky and of things beneath the surface. But do not wonder where the journey leads. It leads you home.

II. The Enemy of Progress

The Lone and Level Sands

Small-souled Napoleon, brooding in Paris, pondered the rich plum of England. It was a fruit he deeply desired, but with Nelson roaming the seas he could not pluck it directly. Were there oblique means? He considered India—its wealth poured into England's coffers—and concluded that it was probably pluckable. But India was a long way off, and Egypt was in the way. First he would have to conquer Egypt.

So in the spring of 1798 the arrow of France was pointed toward the Nile, and cocked, and shot; and thus it was that, on an unrecorded day sometime in 1799, some unrecorded French grunt, digging a trench through unrecorded sands a few miles northeast of Alexandria, felt his shovel fetch up against something hard. Scraping off the sand, he found himself in the presence of a sinister-looking, polished stone tablet about the size of a large coffee table, black as doom and covered with funny writing. He called over his commanding officer, one Bouchard (or Brouchard—no one seems sure), and he in turn called over one of the baggage of egghead scientists the Mad Corsican had insisted on attaching to the Egyptian column; and in this manner the Rosetta Stone, after two long millennia beneath the desert, came once more into the hot, dry light of a Middle Eastern day.

French ownership of the Stone was short-lived. In September, 1801, Napoleon—who, in three years of trying, had never achieved more than a tentative toehold at Alexandria—gave up his eastern adventure and ceded full rights over Egypt and all things Egyptian back to the detested English. The French sailed home. The Rosetta Stone was hustled to London and bundled into a back room at the British Museum.

Sixteen years passed.

In November 1817 the museum finally got around to mounting a display of its Middle Eastern antiquities, and the British public got its first full look at ancient Egypt. The British public proceeded to go gaga. Parties took on Egyptian themes; scarab necklaces decorated the snowy bosoms of every sweet young thing in England. The staid museum became a watering-spot. Throngs poured past the Rosetta Stone daily, through the rest of 1817 and on into the cold winter of 1818.

Amid these throngs, one day near Christmas, strolled a pair of bored young poets. One was a steady, competent sort, the type who wins schoolboy prizes and is immediately forgotten; the other was a dissolute 25-year-old baronet whose work showed flashes of genius, but who had been spending less time on literature, lately, than on radical politics and on the *ménage à trois* he had set up on a suburban estate with his new wife and her fifteen-year-old half-sister. Leaving the exhibit, jolted briefly back into poetry by the dark Presence of the ancient stone tablet, the dissolute young man proposed to the competent one that each of them should construct a sonnet on what they had just seen. The competent one agreed, and quickly produced—well, the anthologies have mercifully passed it by. The dissolute one wrote this:

I met a traveller from an antique land
Who said: Two vast and trunkless legs of stone
Stand in the desert. . . . Near them, on the sand,
Half sunk, a shattered visage lies, whose frown,
And wrinkled lip, and sneer of cold command,
Tell that its sculptor well those passions read
Which yet survive, stamped on these lifeless things,
The hand that mocked them, and the heart that fed:
And on the pedestal these words appear:
'My name is Ozymandias, king of kings:
Look on my works, ye Mighty, and despair!'
Nothing beside remains. Round the decay
Of that colossal wreck, boundless and bare
The lone and level sands stretch far away.

It is 175 years less three months since the Rosetta Stone goaded Percy Bysse Shelley into producing the most universally admired sonnet since Shakespeare compared his Dark Lady to a summer's day, and we are climbing a mountain trail in Nevada, surrounded by limber pine and talus, looking out over Utah. The air is a little thin—we are well over ten thousand feet up—and I find myself pausing often for breath. The strap of the bag carrying my camcorder and tripod cuts into my right shoulder; the bag itself bumps awkwardly against my left hip. A 35mm Minolta SLR dangles before my chest. It is a lovely September morning in the middle of the Great Basin, blue and green with just a touch of autumn gold. A perfect day to visit the site of a murder.

We won't see the corpse, of course. The murder is twenty-nine years old, just the age Shelley was when he drowned in the Bay of Naples. We won't even see the exact scene of the crime—this trail does not go directly to it. Probably the Forest Service, which built the trail, was too embarrassed. The trail became Park Service property when Great Basin National Park was established in 1986, but the Park Service has not altered its route. Possibly they, too, are embarrassed; more likely they simply do not think the murder important enough to mark. The victim was, after all, only a tree.

The Great Basin is actually not one basin but a multitude of them, flat-floored and dry beneath long, linear mountains, a great wrinkled cloth of a land that covers almost all of Nevada, much of Utah, and parts of Idaho, Oregon, California, and Wyoming. Its name derives from a hydrogeologic anomaly; over all this vast region, no rain that falls ever reaches the sea. The streams come down out of the mountains, pool on the playas, and evaporate. There is a river here, the Humboldt, which rises near the Nevada-Utah border, flows westward ambitiously for 375 miles toward California, and then simply stops. There are immense lakes—Great Salt Lake, Mono Lake, Lake Abert—which, because they have no outlets and must therefore keep all minerals brought into them, are far saltier than the sea. But though it is the peculiar behavior of water that defines this land, the overwhelming impression a visitor gets when driving through it is of dryness. The vegetation is mostly greasewood, shadscale, and sage; when trees do appear they are usually juniper and pinyon, as dry and dusty as the cracked, spare soils they inhabit. The walls of the mountains rise stark and sere from the long, gray valleys between them, high and aloof and as barren-looking as the mountains of the moon. This is an illusion. Leave the main roads, climb the mountains, and you will find the forests: ponderosa and cedar, white fir and Englemann spruce, and finally, just below the timberline, the odd, flexible limber pines we now move slowly among. Above the timberline lie cirques and meadows and lakes and tarns, and above these—thousands of feet, still, above—stand the snow-flecked rock ramparts of the peaks. Clouds of aspen drift over the mountainsides, burnishing them, in the fall, with bands and lockets of gold. The barren approaches belie this scenery, which is the stuff of coffee-table books, as lovely and unexpected as a dream.

But I have not yet told the full story. Between the limber pines and the summits, at certain places, are groves of yet another type of pine, odder even than these strange, short, boneless trees beside us whose living branches can literally be tied into knots. These other pines, as unbending and stiff as the limber pines are flexible, are called bristlecones. They are close relatives of the foxtail pine of the Sierra; they have stood atop these Nevada mountains for millennia; and they are, as far as we know, the oldest complex living things on the planet.

The Rosetta Stone, when it was finally translated, turned out to be quite mundane: a priest's decree, in three languages, proclaiming a series of holidays and feast days for a recently deceased king. This fact is of small importance. The thing that grabs us about the Stone is not the message itself, but the knowledge that this message was placed there more than two thousand years ago by other humans remarkably like ourselves. Human voices, engraved in that hard surface, speak down the centuries. The people have passed, but their works endure. Stone is forever.

Shelley spotted the lie in that statement. Human lives are infinitesimal slices of time, mere nanoseconds on the clock of eternity. Human works last little longer. A king dies, his kingdom dies, even his gods die; a statue lingers for a while, is broken, buried, and eroded, and finally there is nothing. And by the earth's reckoning no time at all has passed. We understand this, but we do not—and perhaps cannot—know it. We are far too vulnerable to know. Tiptoeing back from the raw void of the future, we shelter ourselves among the illusions of the present. What we see, what we make, what we gather around us; surely these must endure forever. A president dies, and his doctor murmurs, *now he belongs to the ages.* A stele is set in the town square to carry the names of our heroes down the generations. But new generations have new heroes, and so the stele is replaced, and the replacement is replaced, each one newer, each one better, and each one sure to last forever. The present is a tyrant to which we bow, accepting its yoke, always certain that the trade-off is worth it; that this time, our time is for all time. Each generation thinks this anew, but each is equally wrong. We believe that what we build, for good or for ill, will surely change the cosmos. But our ziggurats last no better than the Babylonians'.

> *Round the decay*
> *Of that colossal wreck, boundless and bare*
> *The lone and level stands stretch far away.*

The rock under my feet is quartzite, a bright, heavy stone, fine-grained, hard, but brittle. Uncountable millions of years ago there was a completely different range of mountains here. Grain by grain, those mountains were converted to sand and carried by wind and water into a sea. The sea evaporated; the sand remained, cemented now into sandstone. The sandstone was buried. Deep in the earth, heat and pressure worked on it, altering its texture from granular to massy, hardening it, contorting it. More heat and pressure cracked the earth and forced what was now quartzite upward. The present mountains rose. Ice formed at their summits, advanced, retreated, and advanced again, not once but many times. Roughly 10,000 years ago it retreated for what we choose to believe was the last time. And only then, after the last ice, came the shapes that are familiar to us, the ones we are now certain will last "forever." In truth, of course, all things that we cherish here—these lands, these lakes, these flowers—will last no longer than any of the stages that preceded them. And whatever we may do to the peaks cannot outlast the peaks themselves. Much as they may concern us, the damages we do are fleeting irritants, as brief as the lives of mosquitoes and about as meaningful.

Still, it was murder. I don't think we can get around that.

The trail begins at Wheeler Creek Campground, climbing a rough moraine through a dark Hansel-and-Gretel forest of Englemann spruce. Half a mile or so from the parking lot it branches, the right fork continuing toward Lake Teresa, the left rising quickly out of the spruce onto an adjoining ridge. Here it enters the limber pine and talus. Trending at first slightly north of east, then east, southeast, and finally due south, it noses around the ridge into Wheeler Cirque. The summit of Wheeler Peak appears, massive and dark, the cliffs of its northern face shooting vertically upward 2000 feet above their hidden base at the cirque's head. And here at last are the bristlecones. The heart skips a beat. The altitude, of course. But is there any forest, anywhere on the planet, anywhere in time, odder or more beautiful than this?

Here is the scene. The cirque is floored by an immense tangle of angular rocks, ranging in size from a child's fist to a small apartment building, but averaging roughly in the range from console TV to grand piano. Out of this wreckage of stone, at widely spaced intervals, rise the trees. They are tawny and squat—as broad, often, as they are tall—and they look much like stone themselves. Most carry only a few sprigs of foliage. There is no underbrush, only the sunny boulders and the sunny, boulderlike trees and, off to the south, the shadowed face of the mountain climbing halfway to the apex of a sky that looks like the raw edge of space. At a few sheltered spots along the base of the cirque's west wall, small groves of tall, slender spruce cling precariously to tiny patches of soil.

The bristlecones are old—incredibly, incomprehensibly old. We think of the time of Napoleon and Shelley as very long ago, and in human terms it is: I am a grandfather, and those were the days of my grandfather's grandfather's grandfather. But when the Rosetta Stone was found, these trees were already extremely ancient. When the Rosetta Stone was *lost*, many of them were already ancient. 2500 years—two and a half millennia—is not an uncommon lifespan here. One trailside individual, which we shall pass in a few minutes, has a verified age of 3200 years; and since verification is difficult (one can only count the rings one can find), its actual age is probably three to five hundred years more. When this tree sprouted, Tutankhamen had not yet ruled, Stonehenge was young, and Moses had not led the Israelites out of Egypt. It was seven hundred years old before Rome was founded, a thousand years old before Plato was born, fifteen hundred years old—a millennium and a half—before the Star shone over Bethlehem. Like Shelley, we have met a traveler from an antique land. And yet compared to some of its kind it is a mere stripling. Elsewhere in this grove, for instance . . .

But that was the murder victim. We are not ready to talk about it just yet.

It would seem incredibly difficult, at such an extreme altitude, to reach such an extreme age. A dendrologist will tell you, though, that this harsh location is actually the key to the trees' longevity. They have climbed above most of their competitors; their enemies are few. Even bacteria do not seem able to reach them. Bacteria have trouble at this altitude anyway, what with the ultraviolet rays and the cold, and the bristlecones' wood is so dense and resinous—a result of exceptionally slow growth, brought on by the same extreme circumstances that slow the bugs—that the attenuated bacteria simply cannot digest it. Bristlecone wood does not rot, it erodes. Wind-driven sand and ice particles abrade it, smoothing and shaping as if with a sculptor's chisel. Each tree is a ventifact, a carved and sanded work of the wind's art, one narrow strip of living tissue growing like a vine on its own exposed skeleton, feeding the needles and keeping them alive. This is what makes a bristlecone grove so incredibly, unutterably beautiful. These are not just trees; they are living statuary.

That is not all there is to it, of course. The slow course of their lives helps their survival in many ways besides simply granting them immunity to bacteria. Slow metabolism means they need less water and less food. Slow growth gives them time to adjust to changing climatic conditions. Slow growth may extend their lives simply because it is slow. The needles of most conifers drop off two to three years after they are grown; bristlecones hold onto theirs for twenty to thirty. It is probably no accident that these trees' lives are ten times as long as those of other conifers, as well.

We don't actually know what kills them. Bacteria don't; neither do grazing animals or gophers. There are almost no enemies at this elevation except for elevation itself, and the trees seem able to deal with that. Probably most of them simply wear out. The metabolic clock runs down; cell division slows, and slows, and finally stops. The wind severs the final strip of bark; the living statue becomes a dead statue, still beautiful, but wearing away now instead of forming. There may be no other species in which the natural course of events is for each individual to die of old age, but that seems to be the case here. There is, however, one thing that can always kill a tree—even a bristlecone—prematurely. That thing is a chainsaw.

Summer, 1963. A graduate student from Princeton, who shall remain nameless here (it is not our purpose to cast aspersions on any specific individual), comes to Wheeler Peak to study the age of its glacial features. He notes the old trees growing in the Wheeler Cirque, on what he correctly identifies as extremely fresh moraine. How fresh? The trees should tell him; they could not have begun growing while the glacier was still there. He attempts to age them accurately. As already noted, this is a difficult—in fact, a nearly impossible—task. The graduate student eventually gives up and goes back to New Jersey.

Late July, 1964. The graduate student is back, determined to get the exact age of at least one tree. Concentrating on several which appear older than the others, he attempts to take core samples. He is repeatedly frustrated by the hard, dense wood and by the uneven erosion of the outer layers. But there is one sure way to do the job: section a tree and count the rings directly. He approaches the Forest Service district office in Ely—the mountain is, at this time, still Forest Service property—and requests permission to fell the oldest-looking tree he has found. It is a tree named (many of these trees have been given individual names) Prometheus.

Monday, August 3, 1964. The District Ranger grants permission to cut Prometheus down. He designates a crew of seasoned timber fallers to go with the graduate student and do the actual work.

Tuesday, August 4, 1964. The crew and the graduate student approach Wheeler Peak. The superintendant of Lehman Caves National Monument, at the peak's eastern base—at that time the only Park Service presence in the Great Basin—intercepts them. Overstepping his authority, knowing this, and not caring, the Park Service man orders the Forest Service people off their own mountain. The crew turn around and head back to Ely.

Thursday, August 6, 1964. The crew and the student return, armed this time with direct orders from Humboldt National Forest headquarters in distant Elko: *Cut 'er down.* They park at the Wheeler Creek Campground—the same place we are parked today, perhaps even the same parking space—and carry the chainsaw into the bristlecone grove. The lead faller looks at the tree that the student has identified, walks over to it, lays a hand on one branch. *I am not cutting this tree*, he says softly. The student argues, threatens, cajoles: the faller strokes the tree and does not budge. Once more the crew packs up and head back to Ely.

Friday, August 7, 1964. The crew and the student make a third trip up the mountain, this time with the District Ranger himself leading the van. They carry the saw back to the tree. The District Ranger studies it for a few minutes, takes the saw in his own office-softened hands, and goes to work. It requires a very long time (Prometheus, though only seventeen feet tall, is eight feet through); eventually, though, the job is done and the victim is dead. They section the corpse with the chain saw and the graduate student begins counting rings, using a low-powered magnifying glass. On what had been Prometheus' midsection, eight feet above ground level, he finally gets an accurate count. At that height—almost halfway up the tree—there are 4,844 rings. There are always more rings at the base of a tree than at its midsection, so the tree is obviously older than that. Rounding cautiously upward, the student assigns Prometheus an age of 4,900 years. Privately he states—and others affirm—that the actual figure is probably closer to 5,200. The extra 300 years are not really significant; even if you only accept the face value of the ring count, what we have here is the oldest living citizen of the planet.

Ah. But, of course, now it is no longer living.

I wander among these 3,000-year-old trees, these young whippersnappers, thinking of Prometheus. What a life it must have been, spanning half the time back to the end of the last ice age! Living the summers; enduring the winters. Watching climate changes, ice conditions, the lives of other creatures, flickering past like frames of a videotape on fast forward. Before the Pyramids were begun this tree had already seen at least 400 winters. Its birth predated Abraham, predated Troy, predated even writing and the wheel. It was already ancient while my direct ancestors were still wandering around the British Isles clad in blue paint. Onward a single life, through centuries and millennia, while Egypt rises, Greece rises, Rome rises, emperors and empires come and go, Stonehenge is built, and the Parthenon and the Pantheon, and the Leaning Tower and the Eiffel Tower and the Empire State Building. A being that breathed while agriculture was being invented—yes, trees breathe—now shares the same air as internal-combustion engines and aircraft and DDT. And then human action—all-too-human action—places a period at the end of the story. We locate the oldest individual on the planet, and we kill him (I find I cannot avoid the personal pronoun any longer) simply to be able to prove how old he is.

Beyond the bristlecones the trail continues, diagonaling up the face of a high, steep, barren pile of rock: the highest, youngest, rawest moraine in the Great Basin. We labor to its lip, wander across its broad, flat, chaotic top, and look down the far side onto the thing the mountain hides from all but those who struggle this far. Tucked at the base of Wheeler Peak's precipitous, 2,000-foot-tall north face lies a remnant glacier. The Ice Age has not ended after all.

I stand in the hot sun, surrounded by thousands of square miles of desert, and gaze at the anomalous ice. There is really not much to see. Though it once had the power to shape this cirque, plucking Wheeler Peak away in huge chunks and carrying those chunks northward well beyond the spot where the bristlecones now live, it is much reduced these days, an old soldier living on welfare and waiting to die. There are those who will tell you that it is already dead; that it is no longer a glacier, only a stagnant icefield in the process of melting away to nothing. Others disagree, pointing to the *bergschrund* at the ice's apex—clearly visible from where we stand—and to the crevasses, fifty feet and more in depth, that occasionally open in its dusty surface. Which view is correct? I don't know, and I am not sure that I care, standing here, so close to the place where Prometheus once lived. What I find myself feeling is gratitude that no one has yet discovered a process to determine the age of glaciers by melting them.

The tyranny of the present rules us all, and all of us react to it. As we cannot conceive of our own deaths—of not-being—so we cannot conceive of the death of our civilization. We put our faith in progress. Earlier ages have fallen, but surely our own is immortal. So Ozymandias built his statue, and so we build our skyscrapers and freeways and computers, and none of them lasts forever after all; all fall, fade, and eventually disappear. And someday, far in the future (but not so far, really, in geologic time), a soldier goes out into the lone and level sands to dig a latrine and marvels at the funny writing he turns up.

When we invented agriculture, freeing ourselves from dependence upon the cycle of want that accompanies the seasons, we thought we had freed ourselves from the seasons as well. We were, of course, wrong; the seasons have continued, we have merely been in denial. To maintain that denial, we have lived more and more for the present. And the more we live for the present, the larger it looms, until it takes over the substance of our lives. The clock and the calendar dominate us; the task we are doing *right now* seems the only important thing on the planet. The more closely it is connected with time, paradoxically, the more necessary it seems, as if putting our hands on history will allow us somehow to halt it. And so we come across a very ancient being, and we want desperately to know how ancient he is. That time thing, you know. And we stop a life forever (death really is forever) just to be able to find out precisely when the thing we are stopping got started.

I want to emphasize, here, the difference between living *for* the moment and living *in* the moment. The former is folly; the latter is a thing that wise ones call us to all of our lives. To live *in* the moment is to merge yourself with it, letting time's stream carry you, finding, as your relative motions match, a sense of the timeless. To live *for* the moment is to attempt to grab it and pluck it out of the stream, freezing it in place, not timeless but out of time. You cannot do this. The moment will pass anyway, and you will be left bobbing in its wake, ever more desperate to catch the next one, ever more fully concentrated on finding a way to do so. Eventually this concentration takes over and crowds everything else out. That is how tyranny develops.

We think that mountains do not think, and we are reasonably certain that the fact that this once-mighty glacier has melted back almost to nothing is of no importance whatever to the glacier itself, or to the peak it rests against. We are less certain of trees, even though most of us believe in the necessity of at least some logging to provide the houses we live in and the firewood we burn and the paper we write upon. Did Prometheus know how old he was? Did he know we were killing him? We will not have reached maturity, as a species, until we know that these questions matter—if not to the trees, then at least to ourselves. To ask them is to acknowledge our debt to Otherness. And it is acknowledgment of this debt that gives us our best defense against the tyranny of the present. To multiply debts, paradoxically, is to free yourself a little bit from all of them. Tyranny can be successful only to the extent that it is able to make you believe that you depend exclusively upon the tyrant.

A king dies, and a pyramid is built; a tree dies, and a theory is built. And neither the pyramid nor the theory makes one bit of difference to the dead. We are all immortal, but only for our lifetimes. We think we can outwit this by building for all of time, but all of time is far, far longer than we can guess. And so our lives are still for naught, and our building is for naught, and all the things we have destroyed to do the building have been destroyed for naught. We cannot change this by building larger and stronger. All we can do by that is to increase the futility of the building process.

One more thing to do, and then we can go home. I wish to touch the ice, to lay my hand upon a thing so clearly transient and yet so much older, even, than the oldest bristlecones. We drop over the lip of the moraine, following the rough path downward toward the snout of the glacier.

Halfway down, rounding a large boulder, I am suddenly brought to a halt by a flash of unexpected green. Here in the midst of this lifeless waste of rock, life has found a precarious grip. A ragged patch of grass, smaller than the Rosetta Stone, basks in the boulder's lee; among the protecting grass blades, tiny penstemons and even tinier bleeding hearts flash crimson and lavender. And as I watch these lives, briefer even than mine, flash by, there comes one briefer yet. A small, white-winged moth, blown here by who knows what wind, has found the flowers. It hovers, pauses; a moment passes, and all eternity is bundled in that moment.

'My name is Ozymandias, king of kings:
Look on my works, ye Mighty, and despair!'

Better we should look on our works ourselves. Perhaps, if we really look, we shall know them for what they are; and that knowledge will create far more despair than the universe will ever need.

The Butterfly's Wing

At the piano, playing Bach. Outside, the wind moves bare oak branches under a mottled January sky; if I turn my head from the music far enough, I can see, through the front window, the torn and tattered edge of yesterday's snowfall melting slowly up the southern slope of the mountain across the valley. The piece before me is a fugue—the brooding, pensive, G minor fugue from *The Well-Tempered Clavier*—and the wind's counterpoint seems to blend seamlessly into the composer's. I am not an accomplished pianist, but Bach lies so well in the hand that the aural shape of the work is clear even at a clumsy first reading. The lines of sixteenth notes curl around each other, purring. The subject sings forth. Gravely, ponderously, the oak dances.

In 1685—the year of Bach's birth—Sir Isaac Newton finally completed the mathematical proof of his Theory of Universal Gravitation. The original intuitive flash had come to him twenty years before, but it had taken a while to work out the details. For centuries, scientists had noted that the earth attracts the falling apple; Newton's genius lay in recognizing that the falling apple also attracts the earth. The question of how far each moves toward the other is resolved solely by the difference in their masses. In the case of the earth and the apple, the apple makes all the quantifiable movement; the earth does move in response to the apple's tug, but it is such a small motion that it cannot be detected by any conceivable measuring instrument. In the case of celestial bodies—the earth and the moon, say—the relative motions are more balanced, and more observable. Planets and moons and comets and asteroids are continually falling toward each other and toward the sun. The complex, interactive fugue of their flight paths resolves itself into the interlocking orbital systems of classical celestial mechanics. Newton found a simple mathematical formula that accounted for almost all observable motion in the heavens, and for the apple as well: the famous inverse square law, $F \mu^{(m_1 \times m_2)}/D^2$, where F is the force of gravity, m_1 and m_2 are the masses of the objects involved, and D is the distance between the objects. (The symbol μ means "is proportional to.")

Almost all. No matter how he worked at it, there remained tiny but measurable discrepancies between prediction and observed reality. For Newton—a deeply religious man—the reason for these was clear. The universe was such a large and complicated place that even God couldn't get it perfectly balanced and running smoothly. The small differences observable between the theoretical and actual positions of the heavenly bodies were the comforting trace of the delicate hands of God, making one of His periodic interventions to assure that everything He had made kept to its proper place in the grand Scheme.

Bach, too, was a deeply religious man. He spent nearly all his creative life in the service of the Church, and every piece of music he wrote—even the nominally secular, such as this fugue my fingers stumble through—was dedicated to the task of glorifying God. Like Newton, Bach was attempting to model the universe as he understood it. In some ways he did a better job. Music is an art, not a science;

it is not as mathematically precise nor as rigorously demonstrable as classical physics. But neither, it turns out, is the universe.

The oak is part of the evidence. Leafless, elemental, reduced to a winter skeleton, it weaves its dance against the January sky. Viewed as a whole, the oak's crown is an immensely complex structure—a great, irregular ball of angled twigs and branches crossing each other in random, chaotic patterns, its shape continually stirred and mixed by the wind. Viewed as parts, though, it quickly sorts itself out. The oak really has only one trick in its bag. The thick trunk comes up out of the ground, rises about eight feet above the matted periwinkle growing about its base, and bifurcates, sending off a heavy branch on the east side. A foot or so higher it bifurcates again; this time, the branch heads off to the northeast. This process continues for several more cycles, each new limb angling out at a slightly different compass direction from the others. Eventually, fourteen feet or so above ground level, the bifurcation produces two equal branches, neither of which can properly continue to be called a trunk; both of these lead nearly straight up. Each splits again a foot above the crotch, creating a quatrain, a poem in wood reaching like a four-armed Shiva toward the heavens. The bifurcations bifurcate; the branches sprout sub-branches, the sub-branches split in turn, limb into bough into shoot, right out to the pencil-sized twigs that meet the wind at the crown's boundary. Thus the tree creates itself from a series of simple Y's, all closely similar, none identical. A single pattern with infinite permutations. Iteration, varied.

Like the fugue. Bach, in company with all musicians worth hearing more than once, creates immense complexity out of elemental forces. A few simple motifs—sometimes only one—varied subtly at each new hearing. The music is in the variations, not the motifs. As Sigmund Spaeth pointed out long ago, Handel's *Hallelujah Chorus* and Frank Silver and Irving Cohn's annoying little novelty tune "Yes, We Have No Bananas" start with precisely the same musical gesture. Beethoven took four notes, three Gs followed by a single E-flat, which may or may not have represented fate knocking at the door, and from these constructed his entire Fifth Symphony. The work, as it unfolds, seems inevitable and predestined, as if its whole shape were latent in those four omniscient opening notes. In a sense, it is. But Charles Ives took exactly the same four notes and came up with the "Concord" Sonata. The immense stylistic gulf between these two pieces is one measure of the power of varied iteration to create large differences from small ones.

The wind that moves the oak is another. Despite our intimate and detailed knowledge of the forces that create and direct the wind—heat differentials, air-pressure gradients, the Coriolis force—it remains a stubborn symbol of capriciousness and unpredictability. Meteorologists once believed that, if they made their atmospheric models complex enough, they could eventually account for all the forces acting within any given air mass and thus predict the weather exactly, weeks or even months in advance. They now know that they were wasting their time. Weather is *inherently* unpredictable. The problem does not arise from the atmosphere's complexity; it arises from the means by which that complexity itself arises. Simple patterns, repeated endlessly, never exactly the same. Iteration, varied. Alter one pattern, even by the smallest amount, and all the subsequent patterns dependent upon it also alter, magnifying the change until the entire structure unravels and recreates itself into something totally new.

Begin the fugue. The subject speaks, spare and introspective, naked as a branch of a January oak. The subject again, transposed and modified this time, and balanced by a line of contrasting counterpoint—a second branch blown across the first, creating new patterns against it. A measure of exposition, all its material derived from one brief moment in the subject. The branches bifurcate again; a third voice joins, then a fourth. A longer exposition this time. Bits of the subject shift and move against each other in the wind of the music, creating new overlays, shaping new patterns. Like the oak, the fugue grows and flowers.

In 1963, a meteorologist named Ed Lorenz sits down at a computer in Massachusetts. Put off by the complex equations of his colleagues, he has decided to try modeling the weather as simply as possible. He feeds three short equations for describing the movements of convection cells in fluids into the machine, sets the equations to altering each other's inputs, loops the program, and waits. Complex waves of atmospheric detail evolve and grow in the output. A particular set of simulated weather patterns intrigues him; he decides to run that part of the model again. Reading the values of all the variables exactly as the machine spits them out back at the point where the pattern he wants to reconstruct begins—precisely identical data, fed into precisely identical equations at precisely the same spot—he restarts the model and goes out for a cup of coffee. By the time he comes back, the output of the second run has diverged so far from the output of the first that it is no longer recognizable as the same experiment.

Laboriously, Lorenz checks everything—first the computer itself (running perfectly), next his input (accurate), then the programming of the equations (correct), and the output (properly recorded). Eliminating possible errors one by one, he finally arrives at the reason for the model's perplexing behavior. The program's output is accurate to only three decimal places; it is rounded off in the fourth.

The algorithm rounds up for values of six and greater; it rounds down for values of four and less. For values of five it flips a figurative coin. It is the tiny amount of randomness that this coin flip introduces, in the fourth decimal place, roughly once each ten runs of the model, that has produced the massive discrepancies observed in the simulated weather showing up at the program's output.

When tiny differences in the starting or operating conditions of a system produce large and unpredictable differences in the result, scientists call the system "nonlinear." Staring at his graphs, Lorenz realizes that he is looking at the first hard evidence for the nonlinearity of global weather. In such a system, he muses, long-range forecasts are chimeras. A tiny displacement of air—a butterfly's wingflap—and a month later the whole dynamic of the global atmosphere might be different. Or it might not. The only way to know for sure would be to chart the location, speed, and direction of movement of every molecule in the atmosphere at the precise moment the butterfly decided to stretch, and for every moment thereafter. Skipping even a single molecule—generalizing by even the slightest amount—could introduce a potentially devastating error.

The data have been graphed as a series of lines—the values of the variables shared among the three equations plotted against time. The meteorologist regraphs it onto a plane. A curious figure emerges: two groups of roughly concentric ellipses, one skewed to the right and the other to the left, joined by a thick, thorax-like line along their common edge. This odd structure, it will eventually be recognized, is a pioneering example of a newly discovered class of mathematical objects, the type now termed "strange attractors." The one Lorenz found is called, quite fittingly, the Lorenz Attractor. Perhaps not coincidentally, it looks exactly like a butterfly.

Iteration; nonlinearity. Bach and oaks and butterflies. I am midway through the fugue, now, and it is becoming more difficult to keep track of what is going on. Back at measure twelve there was a cadence and a short pause for breath, the music reducing itself once more to elementals; but the respite was brief. Now four independent lines of counterpoint are flinging themselves at each other, a sea of sixteenths with the tide rising. The butterfly's wing beats the atmosphere; weeks later and leagues distant, a hurricane rips into Florida. How long is the fugue? Thirty-four measures. How long is each voice? How do we tell? What criteria do we use, and how closely do we look? Do we count notes, or beats? The oak is sixty feet tall. How long is it? Do we measure the twigs, or count them? How many inches do my fingers travel along the keys? Bach is known to have had very large hands. When he played this fugue, was it shorter than when I play it? Is distance objective, or subjective? How long is the eastern boundary of Colorado?

That, at least, we think we know. That is a simple geographical question, and it should have a simple geographical answer. The eastern boundary of Colorado is a straight, mapped line, on the other side of which lies all of Kansas and part of Nebraska. The length of this line, measured out on the ground, is 276 miles. All whole notes and no twigs. Fine. How long is the eastern boundary of Oregon?

This one is a bit more complicated. The straight-line distance along the eastern edge of the state, north to south, is 282 miles; but less than half of that border—127 miles, to be exact, from Nevada up the west side of Idaho roughly to the town of Nyassa—is actually a straight line. The rest of the way north to the state of Washington the border follows the Snake River, and the Snake, though running close to north-south, bends around a bit. A few twigs and eighth notes. Along the river, the 155 straight-line miles between Nyassa and the Washington line stretch out to at least 170. Let us provisionally accept that figure; then the length of Oregon's eastern border can be computed. It is 297 miles. If not precise, that is at least a reasonably accurate estimate. All right, so far. How about North Carolina?

Rain. Although the month was August, and this was nominally the South, it felt like November in Oregon. The night before, in our motel in Rocky Mount, the lights had gone off in the middle of a North Carolina thunderstorm, leaving us floundering about in the dark. The dark appeared to have lodged itself in my soul. For two and a half hours on Highway 64 between Rocky Mount and Nags Head, on the Outer Banks, I had dodged puddles on the asphalt while peering past moving wiper blades. From Roanoke Island, between the Banks and the mainland, two memories stand out: the tiny, earth-walled fort constructed by Sir Walter Raleigh's Lost Colony before it became lost, viewed on the wet run through a curtain of tourists and falling rain; and a fast-food restaurant—I cannot recall which chain—so crowded we finally gave up on it and went out to eat cheese and crackers in the cramped interior of the car, smearing crumbs into the dank upholstery. Now we were forty miles south of Nags Head, on the elbow of Cape Hatteras. The rain was still falling, but we had not come all the way from Oregon just to sit in the car. Grumbling, we pulled on parkas still damp from Roanoke, dodged the lake that had taken over the southeast corner of the parking lot, and stumbled through the wet wind toward the sound of the sea.

Hatteras is an odd—even an extraordinary—place. A long, narrow line of dunes fronted by beach, it lies so far out in the Atlantic that North America seems only a distant rumor. From its heights, which are not very high, you can look either east or west and see ocean stretching from your feet to flat horizon. That is on the part of Hatteras Island north of Cape Hatteras itself, the part where the dunes run north to south. At the cape the Outer Banks kink, and the dunes begin running east to west, along the north edge of the Hatteras Bight. The Cape Hatteras Light stands directly on that 90-degree corner. We had struck the beach to the right of the light, so the sand we strode in the rain was an east-west beach, and we looked south to sea. The Atlantic was gray, and curtained by rain. Waves boomed on the beach and ran up the sand. A west wind billowed our parkas and drove rain, mixed with minute grains of sand, into our faces. It should have been annoying; instead, it was curiously bracing. The world was not all wet asphalt and crowded, fast-food restaurants after all. Here, and now, it was still elemental, and the elements were in control. My dark mood began to lift.

Moments later, it shattered completely. A speck appeared far down the beach to the west; rapidly, it resolved itself into a bird. A big bird, flying low. Long, pointed wings held in a V, it skimmed just above the water, its beak open, the lower mandible cleaving the white surface of the rift as it surged up the beach in front of the breaking surf. Identification was easy, even without a field guide at hand. Though I had never seen a member of its species before, there was only one bird that this could be. *Rynchops niger.* The black skimmer.

We watched, entranced, while the skimmer made several runs. Each run followed the same pattern. Head down, wingtips flapping unevenly but precisely, it steered a course near the moving edge of the rift, parallel to and about six feet in front of the breakers. The open beak clove the flowing foam. The depth of the beak's immersion stayed remarkably consistent; only once did we see it catch on the sandy bottom, racheting rapidly backward and forward again as the bird raised itself above the beach just high enough for the beak tip's arc to clear and then settled down to continue its barely interrupted run. More often the beak would snap briefly shut and the skimmer would swallow whatever it was that it had caught. Each run ended against the lighthouse and its breakwater; the bird would pull up and circle to its right, swinging out to sea for the return flight to its starting point several hundred yards to the west. There it would wheel down to the beach and start the process all over again. These starting and ending points were always the same, as was the bird's behavior between them. It took several of those identical runs before I realized the obvious; they weren't identical at all.

The skimmer flew the same pattern before the waves each time. But the waves were different. Each curl of water breaking upon the beach followed a slightly different course up the sloped sand and back again. The sand itself shifted; its microtopography was never the same for two successive instants. In that wavering world, the bird's flight path had to waver, too. You could predict its northern limit—the line of wrack marking the upper edge of the rift zone—and its southern limit, the line of breakers. You could not tell, within those boundaries, exactly where it would go. Not until it went there. And you couldn't say how far it flew, either. Because each run followed a different path, each run would also be a different length. You could average them, and thus get a figure that pretended to mean something. You could work that average out with great precision—to fifty decimal places, or even a hundred. It wouldn't matter. The next wave up the sand would change it anyway.

How long is the eastern boundary of North Carolina? It varies every second. It varies with the surge and recession of the surf; it varies with the state of the tide, and with the movement of sand in the shore drift. It varies with the length of your ruler. Measure it with survey points a mile apart, and you miss every cove and bay less than a mile wide. Measure it with a yardstick, and you miss the scallops at the edge of the rift. Measure it with calipers set a millimeter apart, and you still miss the tiny fingers of ocean that flow up and spread themselves between the sand grains. You can, of course, say, well, gee, there is a limit to how far we should take this stuff. We should set a minimum grid size and a determinable line on the sand and stick to them. Meters measured along the mean high-tide line will work. You can make that survey, and you can call the figure you come up with the length of the boundary. But every flight of a bird up the beach will call attention to your lie.

Nature, thank God, is messy. It breaks all the rules we set for it. It is endlessly repetitive, but it is simultaneously endlessly varied. It changes as we watch. The neat, clockwork universe of Newton can help us understand it, but it can never precisely match it. Always there remains a screen of abstraction, beneath which Newton cannot penetrate. And it is beneath that screen that the real business of the cosmos is carried on. The butterfly beats its wing at odd moments, sending off strange attractors. The world we think we know dissolves. The surf rolls in and the skimmer finds the edge of it, that much is dependable. Everything else is an oak in the winter wind. Dancing.

Measure 28. For the last three measures the music has settled down to dependability, alternating sixteenth note patterns in the two upper voices scrolled out over material derived from the subject in the bass, the tenor gone altogether. A lull in which we think we know. But now comes the stretto. The butterfly's wing beats once, twice, three times; subjects wheel and spin out from the wing-beats, overlapping each other in tight formation. The music expands to four voices, then to five. The lines are simple—

descending scales, rising seconds and thirds—but they blend chaotically. Dissonances bloom and burst like ripe fruit. Tumult, cacophony; then, like a shaft of light, an immense, ringing G major triad, and the fugue closes. The theoreticians of the Baroque called this sudden appearance of a major third at the end of a minor-key work *tierce de Picardie*—the Picardy third. They thought of it, as they thought of so many things, in theological terms, the dark earthiness of the minor giving way to the radiance of a major-key heaven. Perhaps they were correct. In the meantime, we shall take such weather as we get. The oak moves; the bird flies. Nature repeats itself endlessly and minutely, but it is never the same. After Bach and Hatteras and butterflies, neither am I.

The Thing He Loves

Here is the picture. I am sitting beside a mountain lake, nearly a mile above sea level, at the approximate center of one of the largest national forests in California. Although I cannot see it from where I sit, I know that the surrounding peaks include at least one whose snow-flecked granite summit tops 11,000 feet. The forest around me is composed primarily of ponderosa pine and silver fir, with much Pacific dogwood in the understory. The dogwood is in bloom; its large, creamy flowers with their faint red stigmata—borne, some say, in sympathy with the bleeding Savior—float like a bright fog near the forest floor. The limpid waters of the lake lap quietly nearby. I sweep my eyes slowly along the far shore and spot perhaps 200 large, expensive-looking houses. This is Lake Arrowhead, in the San Bernardino Mountains above Los Angeles, and virtually every square inch of its small watershed is privately owned and bristling with buildings and "No Trespassing" signs. The lake is advertised as a tourist attraction, but there is next to no way a tourist can actually do anything with it. I am sitting, Big Mac in hand, at one of the few sites where a nonresident can even approach the shoreline: the outdoor deck behind the local McDonald's restaurant.

How do we get ourselves into these predicaments, anyway?

Gazing out over the lake, I try to imagine the way it must have looked before human artifacts intruded. This is, of course, futile—the first human artifact to intrude was the lake itself. Arrowhead is an impoundment, created in 1922 behind a dam thrown across a creek called Little Bear, and its primary reason for existence has always been developed recreation. At first this only meant lakeside cabins in the pine forest. Then came a few year-round dwellings, and a few small businesses to serve them. Sometime in the 1940s Los Angeles society discovered the place, winding up the Rim of the World Drive over the 5,000-foot-high face of the San Andreas Fault, and the tone proceeded to go upscale. The camel had put its nose under the tent, and before long the whole beast was inside. What you will see when you go to Arrowhead today is a ring of majestic lakefront dwellings kneeling shoulder to shoulder along the water, like regal elephants. Behind these are several concentric rings of other dwellings, proceedingly less posh as you get further from the lake, although even the least of them is pretty trim. At some point on the hillside the view lots take over and the level of ostentation starts going back up, culminating eventually in a small number of extraordinary hill-top manses. You would probably recognize the names of many of the owners.

Driving around the lake a few minutes ago, I could find only three breaks in this pattern. The first was a tiny, apparently nameless park on the east shore; it was surrounded by a wrought-iron fence and guarded by a big black-and-white sign whose message shouted

WARNING!

*This property maintained for the exclusive use
of Arrowhead Woods residents only.
Trespassers will be prosecuted.*

The second was the village of Blue Jay—a small, fairly conventional-looking business district buried well back in a tributary canyon on the west side of the lake, far away from the water and thus permitted to be real. The third is right here, and it is something else. A town of barely six thousand residents with its own large Hilton hotel. A promenade lined with small specialty shops, like an open-air mall or the concourse at a world's fair designed for the upper crust. A handkerchief-sized park with the lake on one side and the expensive shops crowded around on the other. And this McDonalds, with its low profile, its subdued yet elegant golden arches, its bi-level deck overlooking the water, and its floating dock for the Beautiful People to pull their boats up to. The place is called Arrowhead Village. A single parking lot serves most of the complex, and there is a black man in dark gray livery out in the center of it with a broom. Sweeping.

Now, it is easy enough to disparage all of this. Easy to speak grimly of capitalist excess; easy to make fun of the slick brochures with their breathlessly misspelled descriptions of Yuppie Heaven (". . . a mirror lake of beautiful blue set in a valley inhabited by friendly wildlife, which you will catch peaking at you from behind a pine or boulder. . . ."). Easy, but ultimately unfair. The "mirror lake" may be disfigured with the spiderweb cracks of speedboat wakes, and there may be far fewer Bambis and Thumpers peeking at you (or peaking at you) than there are security cameras, but we are well within the limits of standard advertising hyperbole here, and though capitalist excess has clearly contributed to the near-total demise of natural values in the Arrowhead basin it is not the primary culprit. Arrowhead did not get this way because of the evil lurking in the hearts of industrial barons. Bad intentions are not necessary to achieve bad results. Before you speak too bitterly of the uncaring marketplace and of real-estate developers with dollar signs in place of their eyeballs, perhaps you should take a moment to recall what your grandmother told you about the character of the pavement on the road to Hell.

The dogwood is lovely in bloom. I can see very few dogwood trees from this deck behind the McDonalds— there is one in the tiny park at the other end of the promenade, and a few others have been left, or replanted, by landscapers in yards near the water—but the Forest Service campground back where the road first enters the basin is full of them. The campground is in fact called Dogwood. My tent is pitched in a copse of pines, because that is what was available; but there is a splendid specimen of *Cornus nuttalli*—the scientific name bestowed on the tree by John James Audubon in 1836—only a short distance downslope.

In the spring of 1834, a bored ice merchant named Nathaniel Wyeth began running around Boston attempting to recruit volunteers for an expedition to the Oregon Territory. One of those who answered his call was an odd duck from Harvard University named Thomas Nuttall. Trained as a printer in his native England, Nuttall had emigrated to America in 1808 and had immediately become intrigued by the local flora and fauna. Within five years he had made himself enough of an authority on the subject to be named a Fellow of the august Linnean Society of London; within fifteen years, he had been drafted by Harvard to head up its botanical garden. The epitome of the absent-minded scientist, Nuttall lived in a series of one-room flats, dressed in whatever was at hand, shunned society as thoroughly as society shunned him, and spent virtually all his time in his laboratory at the garden, cataloguing plant specimens. But he also had a strong desire to see, and to collect, the specimens in their natural habitats. Traveling mostly on foot, he had already collected all over the east coast and much of the midwest, and had ascended the Missouri River as far as the territory we now call North Dakota. Wyeth's western expedition was an opportunity for him to collect all the way to the Western Sea.

His party followed what had become the standard route, up the Platte, through South Pass, and down the Snake and Columbia rivers, with Nuttall collecting hungrily all the while. By the spring of 1835 they were at the Columbia's mouth. Here the botanist's attention was caught by a tree with immense showy blooms, clearly related to the flowering dogwood of the east, but half again as big. The flowers and leaves were bigger, too. Specimens of those flowers and leaves quickly made their way into his collecting bags, where they survived unscathed around Cape Horn (Nuttall was by now far too heavily laden to go back to Boston overland), showing up in Boston with the botanist himself sometime early in the summer of 1836.

Shortly after Nuttall's return, Audubon came calling, and the botanist let the dogwood out of the bag. The painter admired the plant, but his real interest lay in the more than 100 bird skins which Nuttall—who also had an interest in ornithology—had managed to bring east with him. Most of these, like the dogwood, were species new to science. Audubon began slavering—and dickering. By October he had 99 of the mounted skins in his possession and was busily adding their portraits to the second volume of his monumental *Birds of America*.

John James Audubon was no scientist, but he was a stickler for detail. Each bird he painted had to be shown life-sized, accompanied by a type of vegetation with which it would normally be seen in the wild. It must have come with a sense of some relief, then, when Audubon—painting the band-tailed pigeon that Nuttall had brought back with him from somewhere near the mouth of the Columbia—remembered the huge flowers of the new dogwood species the botanist had shown him a few months before. He added them to the pigeon's portrait. Researching the tree later for the paintings' accompanying texts, he found that no one had yet given it a scientific name. And that is how *Cornus nuttalli*—*Cornus* from the Latin *Cornu* ("horn"), for the tree's hard, tough heartwood; *nuttalli* after its first, and probably oddest, scientific collector—found its way into the botanical literature.

It is a spectacular plant. The individual I am looking at now, perhaps 300 feet away across the water of this small cove, is typical: a young tree, twenty feet tall and eight inches thick at breast height, its round crown literally covered with white blooms six to eight inches across. Their broad "petals," four to six in number, are veined lightly in green and touched with just a hint of scarlet near their tips. I put the word "petals" in quotes because—as is often the case in nature—things here are not quite as they seem. Dogwood flowers have true petals, but they are microscopic in size. The flowers themselves are tiny and green, and they grow in clusters at the tips of the branches, where they would be virtually invisible if it weren't for their bracts. It is the bracts that we notice. Each dogwood "flower" is actually a flower head, twenty or thirty tightly bunched florets encircled by a ring of from four to six bracts. Individually, no floret is worth looking at twice. Collectively they create one of the loveliest shows in nature.

Biologists have a useful word, *synergy*, which is heard increasingly often these days in lay conversations. The word comes from the Latin *synergismus*, meaning "working together," and it is properly defined as *the qualities of a whole which are not explainable by a study of its parts*. Popular terminology has it as "the whole is greater than the sum of its parts," but popular terminology is a bit misleading here. The whole may just as well be *less than* the sum of its parts. The point is that it is different.

The human body is an oft-cited example. You can analyze its chemical content—so much carbon, so much oxygen and hydrogen, so much water and protein and DNA, and so forth. On a slightly higher level, you can speak of cells of varying makeup, or of the proportions of tissue and bone. You can draw detailed structural diagrams of the skeleton and musculature, of the nervous system, of the circulation of the blood. And nothing you have come up with will ever explain either William Shakespeare or Marilyn Monroe. Or, for that matter, Jack the Ripper. Or you. Or me.

Another standard example is dirt. It is possible to take a spadeful of soil from your back yard and analyze it for chemical content, soil moisture tension, pH, types and numbers of microorganisms, and any other measurement you care to make. It is not possible to use the recipe you come up with to put the soil back together again after you are through analyzing it. The synergy—the *soilness*—will be missing, lost as you broke the connections among the components during the process of analysis, and impossible to build back in. The overall quality of the soil is a result of its evolutionary history *in situ* as much as it is of the actual physical and chemical components. It is a function of the whole, not of the parts. Under analysis, your reconstructed soil may be impossible to tell from the real stuff, but plant a seed in each and you will soon know which is which.

And then there is the bloom of the dogwood. The small, undistinguished and indistinguishable florets. Each bract, a wayward, discolored piece of the sheath that enclosed the developing bud, folded back and afflicted with gigantism. Individually, nothing much to be proud of. Together, a symphony.

There is synergy in human affairs as well, though we rarely call it by that name. A team of individually mediocre basketball players wins a championship, and we speak of the "chemistry" among them which made it possible. The notes of the chromatic scale may simply be played one after the other, or they may be arranged in a multitude of other ways, many of which will flower into music—anything from Bach's B minor Mass to Bobby Darren's "Splish Splash." The words on this page may be displayed alphabetically, or they may form the sentences that give meaning to what you are reading. Try this:

> *and beginning created earth God heaven In the the the . . .*

And now this:

> *In the beginning God created the heaven and the earth . . .*

We call the difference "grammar." It is really just another form of synergy.

So far, all the examples of synergy we have presented have met the popular definition of the word: the whole has always been greater than the sum of its parts. (Well, almost always, anyway. There was Jack the Ripper—and I have a few reservations about "Splish Splash.") Here is an example where the whole is *less* than the sum of its parts: the cruise-control buttons on the steering wheel of your car.

Just over a year before this trip to Arrowhead, I purchased my first cruise-control-equipped car. I am a person who reads manuals, so when I brought the car home for the first time I carried the books I found in the glove box into the house and plowed dutifully through them. Most of the instructions they gave were either insultingly obvious ("to stop, apply the brakes") or forgettable (sorry, I can't remember any of those); but there was one odd phrase which snuck into my mind and stuck there, nagging. It came from the section on how to use the cruise control, and it said, "Set your speed a little slower than the flow of traffic."

There was something vaguely unsettling about that advice, but I couldn't put my finger immediately on what it was. It was only much later, when the phrase popped into my mind as I was going into cruise on one of those long, straight stretches of western interstate where "a little slower than the flow of traffic" is roughly comparable to the lift-off speed of a Lear Jet, that it hit me. Suppose everyone did it this way?

Assume, for the sake of argument, that every car on the freeway has cruise control and that every driver follows, to the letter, the instructions in the owner's manual. Whatever the speed of the flow of traffic, we each set our own speed slightly below it. Fine—but since everyone has just slowed down, the flow of traffic (being the average of everyone's speed) has slowed down as well. We will all have to reach for the "coast" button and lower our speeds a little bit further to compensate. Which, of course, makes the flow of traffic slower yet. The ultimate, inescapable result of this pattern is a large group of cars creeping along the freeway at just over thirty miles per hour, which is as slow as most cruise controls will allow you to go. Independently, our actions have all been impeccably logical and self-beneficial, unquestionably the most sensible thing to do under the circumstances. Collectively they have created an illogical, non-beneficial result, one that none of us who contributed to it wanted at all.

Social scientists call this phenomenon *the fallacy of composition*. Like grammar and music and dogwood blossoms, it is really just synergy under another name. Simply stated, it is this: *things you want add up to things you don't want.* Driving to work adds up to traffic jams. Subdividing farms adds up to the demise of a region's agriculture. Cut one tree down for lumber, and you still have a forest. Cut one more, and one more after that, and one more yet, and pretty soon you have devastation.

And building homes in the woods adds up to destruction of the woods where the homeowners built their homes to enjoy. I think that is precisely what has happened here in the Arrowhead Basin. Each structure—the homes, the Hilton, this McDonalds restaurant, even that immaculate parking lot—can be thoroughly justified on the level of individual benefits. Each makes perfectly good sense— independently. But each also diminishes the collective experience for everyone, *including the individuals who benefit separately.* The act of building a home here unavoidably destroys part of what you have built the home to gain. The whole is less than the sum of its parts. Each individual act may contribute only a tiny bit to the problem, but tiny bits add up. If I adjust my cruise control downward by just two miles per hour every ten minutes, I will drop from sixty-five to forty-five in a little over an hour and a half.

In the 160 years that have passed since Thomas Nuttall and Nathaniel Wyeth set off together to roam the wild, uncharted West, the continent has been almost totally transformed. The scope and the speed of this transformation have been astounding. My father could remember seeing the first automobile arrive in Walla Walla, Washington; he lived long enough to drive a small motor home over the interstate highway system. In my own lifetime I have watched irrigation projects transform much of the arid west from dry pasture to cropland and have seen roads convert most of our forests to tree farms. A few years ago I read Francis Parkman's 1847 book, *The Oregon Trail*, with its lyrical descriptions of vast grasslands, wild buffalo, and travel by horseback among free-roaming native peoples. Several months later I drove eastward down the Platte along the route that Parkman had taken, and all I could think of was how immense was the gulf between what Parkman described and what I saw. In less than two moderately long lifespans we have completely altered the face of North America. Parkman himself saw much of the change: he was a young man when *The Oregon Trail* was published. Before his death he repeated his journey westward, traveling this time by luxury train; a pale wraith of the trip he had taken less than fifty years before. He was not happy. "The sons of civilization," he complained in the preface to the by-then classic book's 1892 edition, "drawn by the fascinations of a fresher and bolder life, thronged to the western wilds in multitudes which blighted the charm that had lured them."

They did not mean to blight that charm, of course. It is important to emphasize this point: no one is to blame here. Individually logical, decent, even compassionate choices have made this illogical, indecent, evil-looking mess of a result. The fallacy of composition has been quite thoroughly at work. "Each man kills the thing he loves," wrote Oscar Wilde, and it is true. I love the wilderness, but every time I go there it becomes less wild, if only by a few more footprints. We cannot stop this from happening; it is a natural force, like time, or gravity. But if we are aware of it we may be able to ameliorate its results. At the very least, perhaps we can stop pointing fingers at each other.

By the time I return to my small, green tent in the pines the evening light has begun to arrive, and with it a threat—or perhaps a promise—of rain. In air beginning to go gray and soft about the edges I walk the Dogwood Trail, a mile-long loop on the hillside below the camp. As the name suggests, there is much *C. nuttalli* here; the large blooms loom in the dusk like the ghosts of ancient moths. There is a smell of earth and pine. Afterward I wander through the campground and across the adjacent high school playing field to the edge of the Rim. A mile below my feet a darkness like purple velvet lies over the Los Angeles Basin, pricked into bewildering geometry by hundreds of thousands of bright, tiny lights. Searching back through memory for the source of my sudden *déjà vu*, I eventually find it: descending over Chicago, by air, at night. Individually, each light is an insult to the unalloyed dark that the wild part of my nature would love to see below me. Collectively, they form what must be among the most beautiful human-made sights on the planet.

Synergy is always with us, for good or ill. Often it seems ill, but it need not be. The dogwood is a lovely reminder; so is this broad, bright dream-catcher at my feet. We make our own destiny, and if we do not always expect what we make, there is still plenty of ground for hope. I raise my arms and hold them out straight from the shoulders, palms horizontal, leaning slightly into the stiff breeze rising up the face of the Rim. Descending over LA, by air, at night. Despite the artifice of the lights and the cars passing close behind me and the pavement under my feet, it is a moment of pure, elemental wholeness. Then I turn and retrace my steps, away from the Rim, back to the noisy fallacy of the filled-up camp.

The Enemy of Progress

Appearances are real but not all that is real is immediately revealed. The real must be unfolded, layer by layer.

— Edward Abbey, *One Life at a Time, Please*

The most completely characteristic thing Ed Abbey ever did was to go out late one June night into the sandstone wilderness of Utah, in the moonlight, and pull up five miles of survey stakes for a new road connecting Arches National Monument to the outside world.

The road was built anyway, of course. Abbey knew it would be; he worked for the same agency the surveyors did. He had seen the maps. If the National Park Service was determined to link Arches to the town of Moab with two lanes of stinking blacktop, the thing was going to be done. You couldn't stop it. But you could put a thorn in its paw. Irritate it a bit; make it think twice before putting the *next* road in. As a Park Service employee, Abbey was charged with protecting the park, and he would do it, even if the agency that employed him was the enemy it needed protection against. "The survey crew had done their job; I would do mine," he would write later. "A futile effort, in the long run, but it made me feel good." Then he went home to the trailer the enemy provided for him and went to bed, outside, under an enthusiasm of desert stars.

Edward Abbey is the most difficult of our environmental saints. Crusty, cantankerous, suffering fools poorly—and apostles of growth not at all—he yawps on the slickrock like a heatstruck Ginsberg, Cactus Ed, as tough-rinded and prickly as all the other southwestern life forms. Critics called him "the Thoreau of the American West," but he had little in common with that prim and ascetic New Englander. Henry Miller was more like it. Try to imagine the Hermit of Walden channel-surfing through cable TV in a motel in Salinas, California, and muttering darkly to his journal: *I keep hearing about too much sex and female nudity on television; where is it?* Or taking the bundle of cash he earned from books decrying mechanization and economic wealth and the cancerous growth of the human-centered planetary phenomenon he liked to spell "syphilization," and blowing a fair-sized chunk of it on a fifteen-year-old maroon Cadillac convertible (promptly christened "The Pimpmobile"). "I'm becoming just one more cranky, cantankerous, dyspeptic, choleric, poker-playing, whiskey-drinking, cigar-smoking evil old man. The curmudgeon," he noted in 1983, and he added: "Good." Not the man you would be likely to introduce to your wealthy grandmother if you wanted to be sure of staying in the will.

Abbey did share with Thoreau a relentless, impassioned, unequivocating search for Truth, a search in which the natural world was critically important. But their approaches were opposite. Thoreau began with nature and moved inward; Abbey began with himself and moved outward. Thoreau sought the truth of the human spirit, Abbey the truth of the human animal. Thoreau found Transcendentalism. Abbey found the desert.

If you want to understand Abbey, you must go to Abbey's world. Begin at Moab ("nowhere such an ugly town in such a beautiful place") and head north and east, into Cactus Ed's "Arches Natural Money-mint"—now Arches National Park—over the detested road he temporarily de-surveyed through Courthouse Wash. The road begins at the new entrance station a mile or so north of the Colorado River on U.S. 191 and climbs rapidly out of Moab Canyon, switchbacking up the bare Entrada sandstone. The rock is bright orange-red under a brilliantine sky. It is 106 degrees outside on this July afternoon, and when you get out of the air-conditioned car at any of the overlooks the heat hits you like the breath of Hell. You find yourself embarrassingly grateful to old John Gorrie, the physician who built the first mechanical refrigeration equipment, in the veteran's hospital in Apalachicola, Florida, all the way back in 1850.

Five miles or so past the North Park Avenue trailhead, beyond the Courthouse and the Organ and the Three Gossips (or the Three Judges—take your pick), you reach Balanced Rock, an improbably phallic pillar topped by an oversized, uncircumcised *glans*. This was the site of the original Arches entrance station, and over the hill to the left, at the head of the broad wash known as Willow Flats, was the location of Abbey's Park Service trailer—his home for the three summers in the 1950s that were compressed into the single season in the wilderness which forms the scaffolding for *Desert Solitaire*. (The five miles of road you just covered from North Park Avenue was the stretch he made the Park Service survey twice.) Here the road forks: right for the Windows; straight ahead for the rest of the park. Take the right fork first, winding westward past Elephant Butte and the Garden of Eden to a small traffic circle with parking on its east and west sides and a large, upscale, wooden shithouse in the middle. Eastward, beside the bluff, stands the nested, right-angled, twin span of Double Arch; westward lie the Windows, small against the distant La Sal Mountains. Short trails lead in each direction. The hikes are worth the effort, even in this heat; but if you've any doubt about your strength, save it. You can see these particular arches pretty well from the car if you carry a good pair of binoculars (Abbey on motorized visits to Arches: *The tourists drift in and out of here like turds in a sewer. . . . And I? I am a watcher of turds*), and there is a thing later, which you must not miss, that will not be so genial and compliant.

Back to the junction; turn right once more, toward the Big Beyond. Pass Panorama Point (only a panorama) and take the gravel road that splits off eastward a mile or so to the north, curving down into the green sand wilderness of Salt Wash. The sign pointing down this road says "Delicate Arch," and that's where you are heading. But you won't get a view of it from what Abbey called your "iron dinosaur" —not even from a distance. One foot must go in front of the other.

You have two choices. The first is to drive all the way to the end of the road, leave the car in the small, usually crowded parking lot there, and take the trail that begins in the northeast corner of the lot. A short climb over domed ledges of buff-grey Navajo sandstone will lead you to an unsatisfactory view of the arch across a broad, vertical-sided gorge. Lost and small in a large confusion of fins and ridges, it looks a bit like a bow-legged cowboy's chaps without the cowboy. The view gets better as you climb westward up the ridge, but only a little better. A good telephoto lens will give you a decent picture; nothing here will give you a decent sense of the place.

The other choice is the Delicate Arch trail itself. Drive back down the road to the bottom of Salt Wash. Park. It is best to wait until late in the day, 5:30 p.m. or so, when the temperature has dropped into the high 90s. Take water. Take lots of water.

A hundred yards or so beyond the trailhead, you pass a tumble-down cabin on the left. Known as the Wolfe Cabin (or the Turnbow Cabin; it depends on the age of your source), it was the home of a small-time rancher from Ohio who managed to eke out a living running cattle in this place for a couple of decades back in the early years of the century. Just beyond the cabin is clear, tamarisk-shaded Salt Creek, inviting but unpotable; the rancher used it for irrigation, but he had to obtain drinking water for his family and his livestock from a spring half a mile up the valley. The trail leaps the creek on a narrow, swaying suspension bridge, climbs over a low rib of sandstone, and crosses the floor of a dry wash. Here the real work begins. For nearly a mile you will be out in the open, on sloping stone, in the heat. The trail is a few cairns marking a general course west and up. There is no water; there is no shade. There is only you and the rock and each step's insignificant rise and run under the hammer of sky. Take a few steps; pause. Take a few more steps; pause again. Every third pause or so you will find yourself drinking deeply from your canteen. The heat, as much as the exertion, wears you out; your legs begin to go. The slope is long. There is plenty of time to wonder what the hell you are doing here.

Well, what *are* you doing here? Fulfilling some sort of need, obviously; you would not submit yourself to this much torture, on purpose, for mere desire. But what need? Abbey made this trip daily, on duty, six months out of the year for three years; and when he didn't have to do it for his job any more, he came back and did it again. For himself. Several times. Why? It is supercilious, and wrong, to say: Because he liked Delicate Arch. Of course he did, but that is not the answer. Like is not a need. Love is a need; but the kind of love you can say that about is love that can be reciprocated. Love for another person, or for an animal. Love, perhaps, even for a tree. Not love for an odd-shaped rock on the drop edge of nowhere with an access route that feels like climbing the doorstop of Hades. You think about the car's air conditioning. You think about cold beer. You put your booted, sweating foot eighteen inches further forward on the slope. Again.

What do we need? The obvious: breath. Hot air moving in and out of the lungs. Water: we're carrying that. Nearly as hot as the air by now, but wet. In at the mouth, out at the pores. Food: back in Moab, later, as a celebration of survival. Shelter: temporarily gone without. Would be nice. Procreation. Not here, you fool, but isn't it nice what the heat makes women want to do with their clothing? (Abbey: "The tragic fallacy of *Joy of Sex* and all other such training manuals is that what a man really desires is not 144 different positions, but 144 different women." My wife, when told of Abbey's remark, said, "I always knew it. It's only women who are K-selected animals. Men are r-selected." Biologists will understand. The rest of you can look it up.)

None of those needs, though, explain what we are doing out here in the middle of this superheated slab of coarse-grained, buff-colored bedrock. Most of them, in fact, argue *against* it. There is no water here, and no shelter, and we are not on our way to either of these. There might be animals we could catch for food, but not until sunset and then only if we are not overly squeamish. About the only need we have that is satisfied easily out here is the need for air, and we hardly have to fry ourselves like an egg on a sidewalk for that. There must be some need we have not yet enumerated; a strong need, one with enough power behind it that we are willing to undergo extreme discomfort—even the possibility of death (heat exhaustion can easily claim the desert-unwary)—to fulfill it.

The cairns are bearing left, now, into a broad cleft between two low knobs. A little shade if you cling to the south wall, though the gain may not be worth the risk. Hugging that wall a few years ago, I suddenly noticed that pounding my walking staff on the stone beneath my feet produced echoes straight down. How thick was the flake of stone I stood on, and how easily broken, and how far down to the next one, after the obvious air-filled gap? No way of knowing. No real desire to find out. The cleft narrows to a pass. The obvious route is over the pass and down, onto the broad, orange platform beyond. But the cairns lead upward to the right. A narrow, slanting ledge—perhaps natural, perhaps blasted out of the stone—across a face, leading toward a second, higher pass. The way is steep; the drop to your left is dizzying. The view forward is blocked until the very last second; then your eyes suddenly top the pass, and you see

. . .

Many have tried to describe this moment. All have failed. I have no desire to add to the pile of failures. I will state, however, that it is immediately clear that this is what you have come for. The meeting of the need, whatever the need was. The quest fulfilled. And after the moment has passed—after the indescribable has begun to fade, after the sweat and the thirst and the desire for rest and respite have begun to crawl out, once more, from whatever dark recesses of the body they were driven into by the act of fulfillment—it is only natural, if you are a reflective person, to replay the moment in your mind, seeking clues to that still-unidentified but clearly satisfied need. You topped the pass and there, two hundred feet distant across its perfectly carved bowl, was the perfectly carved, impossible arch, poised on the edge of its dropoff, framing the La Sal Mountains. The heart leaped and tingled. What does that? Mozart can do it, or Michelangelo, or the sweet, sudden rush of understanding that comes when you first realize that Euclid was by-God-right. Thelonius Monk's piano. A three-piece sacrifice by Paul Morphy leading to mate in one. The thrill, as a child, of mud, or peek-a-boo, or the headlong rush of a swing toward the ground that ends, not with an impact, but with a swoop, a tangent, and a mirroring rush away. Do you recognize this thing you need yet? It is joy.

Joy, a need? Puritans would hardly agree; but Puritans are out of place in the desert. Abbey, no Puritan, had no doubts about the matter. "Only a fool envies the joy of a child," he wrote in 1987; "a grown-up man or woman shares in that joy." In *Desert Solitaire* he addressed the question more directly:

> *Has joy any survival value in the operations of evolution? I suspect that it does; I suspect that the morose and fearful are doomed to quick extinction. When there is no joy there can be no courage; and without courage all other virtues are useless.*

A full understanding of the radical nature of that passage requires placing it in context. Many people, I suspect, will agree with it as long as those exhibiting the joy are understood to be human. A fair number will continue to agree if it is stipulated that it also applies to dogs and cats and the other "higher" mammals. But Abbey was writing about frogs. And it is only by carrying it that far—that far, or farther yet, to insects, trees, perhaps even bacteria—that you can begin to understand that joy is truly a need, not merely an incidental and transitory phenomenon of the higher brain. Pleasure is intense but shallow; happiness is a moving target which never holds still long enough to reach it. Desire is a social disease. But without joy we die. (Abbey:

"Outdoors! Outdoors! Outlive the bastards! Joy, shipmates, joy! Piss on their graves!")

If I have written the truth, then nature is full of joy. And for this reason, if for no other, nature is a thing we must not waste or tear apart. Because to do so is to destroy joy. And because this act of destruction—like the destruction of air or water or foodstuffs—will eventually turn about and destroy the destroyer. In a finite world, destruction means reduction. You cannot continue to systematically reduce the pool of a resource that you depend upon to smaller and lower-quality amounts without at some point jeopardizing your own survival.

If all this seems more evident here than elsewhere, it may be because the desert focuses it so well. In this harsh, difficult land, needs become highlighted. Where life is reduced to its essentials, those essentials tend to stand out. Water, and the demand for it; shelter, and the demand for that, shadow or cave or air-conditioned car. Food. The desert has few of these things, and hordes the ones it has. But it has plenty of excellent air. And it is chockful, overwhelmingly plentified, with joy. That, in the end, is what brings us here, and keeps us. We push the other needs to the limit so that we can leap, cavort, gambol, luxuriate, swim—perhaps even drown—in this one.

Advocates of economic growth often spoke disdainfully of Abbey as an "enemy of progress." If by this they meant that he was a hairshirt opponent of luxuries, then it must be respectfully submitted that they were all wet. Abbey had a sybarite's respect for luxuries; he just never confused them with needs. And because of this he understood the nature of growth far better than the growth advocates do. Growth expands needs. It is therefore in direct conflict with progress, which consists of improving our ability to meet needs while keeping up as nearly as possible with the human animal's insatiable appetite for wants. Demanding both unrestrained growth and unlimited progress is self-contradictory; it is like screaming for a touchdown while simultaneously moving the goalposts outward faster than either team can run. Abbey on progress:

> If "progress" means change for the better—and I'll support that—then growth as we have come to know it means change for the worse. Let me try out another new-fangled maxim here: Growth is the enemy of progress. Look around you and see what growth has done to your city. . . we live in the age of accelerated growth and diminishing returns.

The human-made environment blunts this lesson. That is why Abbey wanted us out of our cities, and out of our cars. To separate the needs from the wants. For that matter, to separate the needs from each other. To see how deprivation of one need can lead to a heightened satisfaction of the others. How out on the hot slickrock, with no shelter and no food and precious little water, you can suddenly find yourself fulfilled, in a manner both unexpected and inevitable, on a level of completeness that is possible in no other way.

Toward the end of his life Abbey chose as the epigraph to a slim collection of his essays the Prayer of Saint Francis of Assisi, the one that begins: "Oh Lord, make me an instrument of thy peace. . . ." An odd gesture, perhaps, from a celebrated agnostic who called God *Gawd* and was famous for his unabashed advocacy of sabotage as a weapon against environmental destruction; but nearly as characteristic of the man as was pulling up survey stakes in the desert. For Ed Abbey was, at heart, a peacemaker. Do you doubt this? Then go back both to the desert and to St. Francis. See what is common to each. Here, to help you, is Abbey's version of the prayer, lined out as a poem and breaking off in the middle with an ellipsis, as he preferred. Note the precise spot where his ellipsis begins:

> *Oh Lord, make me an instrument of thy peace.*
> *Where there is hatred, let me sow love;*
> *where there is darkness, light; and where*
> *there is sadness, joy . . .*

Hopeful Monsters

On my desk, a few inches from my left hand as I write these words, rests a small sandstone pebble. Plucked from a beach on the northwest coast of Michigan's Keweenaw Peninsula more than a decade ago, it is light tan in color and roughly spherical in shape and looks, at first glance, like a discarded chunk of art eraser. Locked within it are the remains of a dead shellfish approximately 400 million years old.

The creature was a brachiopod, a member of a large and ancient phylum, once numerous, today nearly extinct. Humans have had little to do with this extinction, the greater part of which took place nearly a quarter of a billion years before we came on the scene; primarily it has been a result of habitat change coupled with competition from later, more successful animals. Like mollusks, which they superficially resemble, brachiopods are filter-feeders that live enclosed in a pair of hinged calcium-carbonate shells. Mollusks, however, lie crossways in their shells, while brachiopods lie front-to-back; and this seemingly insignificant difference, along with a slightly greater tolerance for changes in the salt content of sea water, has caused the mollusks to thrive and the brachiopods to fail. The 85,000 or so living forms of mollusks account for from two-thirds to three-fourths of all known species in their phylum; many now dwell in fresh water, and some are even terrestrial. The fewer than 300 living forms of brachiopods account for somewhere between one and six percent of known species in their phylum, and all of them are marine.

My brachiopod fossil is lovely—a nearly complete upper shell, its thumbnail-sized half circle scored with radiating ridges and grooves like a miniature Chinese fan. Near it in the small stone can be seen a concavity where the lower shell may have rested and, edge-on, broken bits of several similar shells. Lovely, but troubling. My colleagues and I in the environmental movement, this winter of 1995, are locked in a bitter battle with developers over the fate of the Endangered Species Act, a piece of legislation designed to prevent extinctions. Emotionally, I think we are correct. It is foolish and dangerous to tatter the pattern of planetary life by casually wiping out whole species of living things, without any attempt to understand where in the web they fit and whether we might not in some way depend on them, on the flimsy excuse of making more money; and even if it were not, we humans have no goddamned right. Death for profit is always an ugly idea, and extinction is the ugliest form of death. But I look at my bit of sandstone, and I am troubled.

Should we really have saved all those brachiopods?

Two weeks ago, prowling the shoreline of the irrigation reservoir called Emigrant Lake a few miles east of my home during an afternoon of casual birding, I noticed that the ducks and shorebirds suddenly became agitated. A moment later the reason became clear. A bald eagle had entered the area and was cruising a lazy circle two hundred feet or so above the muddy water. Only a short time ago that experience would have been impossible; there were no bald eagles near enough. The fact that eagle populations have recovered sufficiently to allow the birds to begin recolonizing my Oregon valley is a benefit directly attributable to the

Endangered Species Act. There are other success stories: the American alligator, the Palau dove, the brown pelican, the whooping crane. I am grateful for their survival. I strongly support continuance of the kinds of efforts which have made that survival possible.

Among the most memorable afternoons of my life was one spent a few years ago in a Louisiana wildlife refuge, watching a trio of roseate spoonbills—another species that almost didn't make it—trolling their big beaks side to side as they walked slowly through feeding patterns older than human knowledge in a small, half-hidden pond forty feet or so off the path on which I stood bathed in an awe every bit as bright and burning as the southern sun.

So it is with great reluctance that I write these next words. But this must be said: the Endangered Species Act is a flawed document, based on a faulty worldview, which seeks untenable results. Like any instrument that attempts to freeze change, it cannot hold. Its goal of halting all extinctions is noble but unnatural. Not all extinctions can be halted. Some extinctions should not be.

Perhaps I ask too much. Perhaps the only way to keep too many extinctions from happening is to attempt to prevent them all; perhaps this imperfect Act is the best we flawed humans can hope to come up with. Perhaps; but I hope with all the urgency I can muster that this is not so. There must be some way to protect those species which clearly need our protection, and yet avoid the hubris which says that every creature we have knowledge of—or might have knowledge of—is thereby blessed, and must go forth and multiply forever, whether or not its existence continues to be necessary, fit, or even desirable.

In all the flap over reintroducing wolves to Yellowstone, with environmentalists pontificating ecological restoration and ranchers screaming shoot-on-sight, I have yet to hear a single voice questioning whether or not the wolves themselves really want to be there.

Northward across 100 miles of restless blue water from the beaches of the Keweenaw, the time-hardened cherts of the Gunflint Formation slope into the Ontario side of Lake Superior. Here and there in these cherts are collections of odd, layered structures of calcic rock, circular in form and from one to three feet in diameter. They are stromatolites, the product of colonial species of blue-green algae, and the discovery of microfossils of the algae themselves in these two-billion-year-old gunflint stromatolites during the 1950s was the first positive proof that life existed in the earth's Precambrian seas. Many others have been found since. The oldest known are from Western Australia; these have been reliably dated to 3.5 billion years B.P. (Before Present). As it happens, Western Australia also contains living stromatolites, perhaps of the same species as the ancient fossils. Perfectly adapted to a specific, limited set of conditions—warm, shallow, highly saline waters—these organisms and their ancestors have watched literally millions of other creatures come and go. Speak the names now. *Trilobite. Dinosaur. Archaeopterix. Pterodactyl.* They roll off the tongue like bittersweet music, each conjuring up images of creatures we love and none of us will ever see. It has had to be that way. Extinction discomforts us; but extinction is the inevitable byproduct of evolution. It is the price that life pays for improved adaptations. Each time a better match for a niche is developed, the species already occupying that niche must be driven out. If it is not, there will be no place for the new species to go.

Nature proceeds in fits and starts and jerks: always has; always will. The gradualists are wrong. Uniformitarianism is real—all natural forces in effect today have always been in effect; all natural forces in effect in the past are still in effect—but it operates in a nonuniform manner. A volcano explodes, or a meteor hits. Rivers abruptly change their courses. The average ambient temperature changes by a few degrees, and ice covers half the planet. The Age of Reptiles ends. Long periods of equilibrium give way to rapid change, then settle back to equilibrium again. Life lives. And living, like it or not, unavoidably includes death.

I am well aware that the current rate of extinction—more than 100 species per day—is unprecedented in the history of the planet. I am equally aware that most of these species are not dying through the traditional means of niche competition, but through the much more drastic mechanisms of niche emptying and niche destruction. These are legitimate grounds for concern. The continuing attempt to remake the entire surface of the earth into a habitat for a single species—ours—is wrongheaded, selfish, and stupid. It is also ultimately doomed. We are perfectly correct in wanting to head off that doom before it encompasses the doomers as well as their victims.

But it is equally wrongheaded and selfish and stupid to say that no existing species should ever die. Extinction is a fundamental natural process. To pass legislation outlawing it is akin to trying to halt the seasons by decree. You can't do it, and even if you could, you probably wouldn't like the results. This whole, huge, dynamic, living, breathing, fighting, fucking planet would become a butterfly in amber—pretty, perfectly preserved, but utterly worthless for any of the things you would normally expect a butterfly to be able to do.

More than fifty years ago, the geneticist Richard H. Goldschmidt coined a term to describe the random mutations that are one of the several means that evolution has for driving itself forward. He called them "hopeful monsters." Monsters because they show traits that did not come from their ancestors—always different, sometimes strange, occasionally bizarre. And hopeful because there is always a chance that these different, strange, or bizzare traits may actually help the creature cope better with its environment, thus giving rise to a new species. It is not a very big chance; even under the best of circumstances, the odds are overwhelmingly against a monster simply surviving, let alone being able to breed and, if bred, to pass on the new trait. Monsters are almost always dead ends. But vanishingly small though the hope may be, it is still hope, and like all hope will occasionally be rewarded.

And these rewards—though always rare—are most likely to happen during periods of rapid environmental change. That is the key point to keep in mind here. When nature is stable and all niches are full, there is no room for monsters, hopeful or not. When things are stirred up, when something like a flesh-covered bulldozer is running amok in the world, emptying old niches and opening fresh ones—when the slow waltz of nature has been pushed into a rumba with noticeable elements of hip-hop—then something new may gain a fingerhold, and the tiny ember of hope may become a flame.

Please understand, I am not suggesting that we do away with the Endangered Species Act altogether. Nor am I in agreement with those who demand that we rewrite it to allow for the consideration of "economic criteria." By this they usually mean that making money must always take precedence over saving species, and this is a selfish, human-centered view, and it is wrong. All I am really saying is this: to demand that all extant species must survive forever is also selfish and human-centered and wrong. Some we do no favor by forcing them to remain, willy-nilly, a part of an ecosystem that no longer has room for them. Some should be allowed to slide gracefully into oblivion.

Which should be saved, and which let go? We have neither the criteria nor the right to judge. Therefore let us not attempt to. Let us stop looking at individual species and concentrate, instead, on habitats. Let us make certain that nothing we do, as a species, fragments any habitat type on the planet beneath its ability to reconnect, shrinks it below viable size, or otherwise prevents it from functioning. Beyond this, let us let nature do her work. Habitats will grow, shrink, change, shift, evolve. Some species will disappear. But some species always have. Life does not come with a guarantee. We have no right to go around randomly smashing our fellow living creatures out of existence. But neither do we have the right to go around injecting them with embalming fluid.

Four hundred million years ago the brachiopods swarmed through the Devonian seas. Today I pick up my small rock. Rounded by the Lake Superior waves, it fits comfortably into the hand. Nothing my reckless species did caused these creatures' deaths. We who have killed so many things cannot count coup on this one. I think of the species we have slain— the dodo and the great auk, the passenger pigeon, perhaps the mammoth, creatures less famous beyond count or telling—and I feel a sense of overwhelming loss. I would do anything to stem the tide. But when I thrust my hands into the sea, the brachiopods are already gone.

On the Edge

Things reveal themselves at their limits. That was why I was sprawled by a small lake just below timberline in the Siskiyou Mountains, physically spent, watching evening alpenglow turn the peak across the canyon a shade of orange so impossibly deep and pure that photographs of it, viewed today, look like blatant lies.

The lake was called Towhead. Less than three acres broad but more than fifty feet deep, it lay cupped like a rainpool on a tiny rock shelf near the head of a precipitous gash in the mountainside known as Hello Canyon. The glowing wall close at hand to the east was the west face of a craggy, twin-summited, buff-red peak with the unimaginative but apt name of Red Buttes; to the west, the equally red cliffs of Kangaroo Mountain rose sharply above tumbled talus. In shadow now, these would have their turn to glow when the sun came up. Southward lay cirques and meadows, stairstepping up over patches of snow and bands of white marble to the canyon's head at Kangaroo Saddle. Northward lay space. Less than thirty feet from the north edge of the lake, the rock forming its shelf came to a lip and stopped, suddenly. Nearly 600 precipitous feet below, the canyon floor began again as boulder-strewn meadows sloping into a larger but shallower lake called Hello. Beyond this lake, Hello Creek plunged and rumpled and sang through its steep, forested gulch, racing its spray toward the Butte Fork of the Applegate, two miles away and three thousand feet further down.

Which explained the part about being physically spent. There is no trail to Towhead, but there is an easy way in: by road to Cook and Green Pass, four miles up the Pacific Crest Trail from the pass to Kangaroo Saddle, then a half-mile ramble down through the meadows to the lake. I hadn't come that way. For various deranged but perfectly legitimate reasons I had begun at the Butte Fork trailhead, hiked the two easy miles up the river trail to the spot where Hello Creek surges loudly out of the forest on the far bank, balanced my way across on a couple of fallen logs, and followed the creek up its horrendously steep canyon to the lake. In the August heat. Carrying a thirty-pound pack. The two miles of near-vertical bushwacking had taken me six sweaty hours. For a young person in prime physical shape the route would have been questionable; for a middle-aged man with a heart condition it was damned stupid. The last half hour, climbing the open rock above Hello Lake, I was in fibrillation, my heart leaping about the cage of my chest like a captive weasel each time I moved. I was hiking solo, miles from any possible assistance. Things reveal themselves at their limits. It gradually occurred to me that I could die.

I watched the terminator creep slowly up the face of Red Buttes. There seemed nothing better to do. Inch by inch up the rough surface, poking into the hollows, extinguishing the bright rock like water over coals, pulling the night behind it. High clouds lit from beneath were dark purple against the sky's deepening blue. I was thirty feet or so above the west shoreline, in the midst of the talus, sprawled on a large, irregular boulder whose flat surface tilted slightly toward the lake. A cool breeze wandered over intermittently from a nearby snowfield, but the stone beneath me still held the heat of the day. Talus, lakeshelf, meadow above and canyon below, were all in shadow. Only the peaks still held the light.

If I could choose my site to die, I suppose it would be someplace like this. Beside a timberline tarn, on glacier-smoothed rock, in the evening. The limits of a day, the limits of a forest, and the limits of a life, converging. The terminator and the Terminator joining hands. Somewhere, in the void beyond the lip, a birdnote. Now I lay me down to sleep . . .

Morbid. I sat up; the weasel grumbled and stirred. I suspected it would get pretty lively if I moved very far, but as long as I remained relatively still I could ignore it. The lake was quiet and dark. In the small meadow near the inlet stream the gray triangle of my tent loomed in the dusk. On first arriving at the lake, in the late afternoon, I had sat for a long time under a lone Jeffery pine on a knob of smooth stone above the outlet stream, mere yards from where the stream became waterfall, waiting for the weasel to leave. When it had become obvious that the critter was planning to stick around for the duration, I had carried the pack slowly around the lake to the inlet meadow and pitched the tent. A spit of rain just as I drove the last stake had sent me inside for a few minutes; when that subsided, I had crawled out and come up here. I had been here ever since.

I looked across the lake to the knob and the lone pine. Jeffery pines look remarkably like Ponderosas, but they have two traits that set them apart from their more common cousins. One is odor; Ponderosas smell like vanilla, but if you place your nose to a crack in a Jeff's bark and inhale deeply you will get a surprisingly strong whiff of fresh pineapple. The other is the places they live. Ponderosas are trees of moderation; they like moderately deep, moderately acidic soils at middle elevations on moderate slopes in semi-arid climates. Jeffs are extremists. They are usually found at or near the timberline, on steep slopes, in soils that no other tree will touch. Often they appear to be growing right out of the rock. The tree across the lake was typical. The glacier that had carved the knob at the edge of the lake's shelf had carried away all the soil it could reach, but the knob had a couple of cracks in it, and a tiny amount of dirt had hidden inside them. The tree had found it. Gripping the rock with roots like claws, it huddled over its little cache of soil and let the timberline winters pound it. Perhaps twenty feet tall, bent and twisted like a magnified bonsai, it might have been as much as 300 years old. On the edge, but thriving.

What drives a tree to grow in such a place? An odd lodging of seed, of course; but surely there must be more. The protoplasm must know its chances. Seed to seedling, seedling to sapling, sapling to young tree; always the extremes of weather, always the thirst, always the rock where questing roots seek soil. Sixty minutes of struggle each hour, twenty-four hours of struggle each day, 365 days of struggle each year; 525,600 chances a year to say the hell with it. Yet the tree lived and grew. Defiance? Optimism? Sheer, raw stupidity? Whatever it was, it was not only this particular tree that had it. Two hundred feet west of its knob, just beyond the narrowest part of the lip, six young Jeffs with straight boles hung their silhouettes like temple pillars against the blue void. Others peered down over the edges of tiny shelves on the cliffs of Red Buttes and Kangaroo Mountain. There were not many, but they reached, at least as knee-high krummholz, all the way to the summits. Up-canyon, punctuating the meadows, dark, dense copses of mountain hemlock somehow managed to shelter each other and survive. The timberline is a limit but, like two-year-olds, trees continually test it. Often they get away with things that by rights they should not.

Like two-year-olds, or hikers with heart conditions. What is this thing we have about limits? We know they exist, and we are pretty good at discerning what they define. What perverse urge keeps us pushing beyond them? Already by the foot of the cliff above Hello Lake I had known I was in trouble. There were perfectly good campsites there—water, views, level tent sites, everything else I needed. What was it that drove me, heart already fibrillating, up the 600 near-vertical feet of open rock beyond?

If there is an answer, I suppose it is simply "life." I breathe, therefore I exceed. Once metabolism has begun, it takes continual acts of excess to keep it going. Oxygen was poison until some early bacterium tried out the Krebs cycle and discovered that it could actually use the stuff. Life was confined to the sea until plants, and then animals, ventured up the frightening slope into the bright and alien air. We are programmed to court failure, because that is the only way to reach success. Like the Jeffery pine, we live continually on the edge. Show us our limits: fine. We enjoy seeing them. But don't tell us we have to stop there.

Limits, of course, are real. Timberline exists; there are no trees of any description anywhere near the summit of Mt. Everest. Vast stretches of the Rockies and the Sierra are totally treeless; so is the north side of the Brooks Range, and most of the Arctic plain, and the entire continent of Antarctica. Much of New Hampshire's Presidential Range rises into tundra, snowy most of the year, swept by winds of startling ferocity, void of any plant more than a few inches tall. Trees truly cannot live in these places. They are tree-lethal. But the only way a tree can learn this is to die.

And sometimes they don't. Sometimes the limits are confounded; sometimes you get a Jeffery pine or a copse of hemlocks. Or a fibrillating heart that shudders and thuds and keeps on beating anyway. This is because limits are fuzzy. They are not porous; they hold. But they hold differentially. For a Jeffery pine less than for a Ponderosa; for a mountain hemlock less than for a Douglas fir. And for some individuals less than others. The genes may tell, or the microclimate. Protected by a rock, a seedling may flourish; armed with greater drought tolerance, a young tree may get through a dry spell that dessicates its cousins and siblings. Without the fibrillation, the fruit of a hereditary condition, I would be merely tired. With it there was a chance—though less and less as time went on—that tonight's sunset would be the last I would see. That these thoughts, which I had not written in my terse journal, would die with the mind that was processing them.

I lay back again on the hunk of talus, hands behind my head. The stone was cooler, now, and the air was chilly even with no breeze. My thin T-shirt—far too warm, earlier in the day—had become inadequate; soon I would have to either put on more layers or go to bed. Or perhaps both. A few more minutes to watch the terminator top Red Buttes, and then I would retire to the tent. And dare the weasel to be there in the morning. Slowly, relentlessly, the shadow line moved up the last few-score feet of the face, gobbling the alpenglow. Another fuzzy limit. Night is real; but where does night start? Tucked under Kangaroo's massive flank, Towhead had been in shade since late afternoon. That was not night. Neither, really, was what I had been calling the terminator. The line closing in on the summit of Red Buttes was not the shadow of the planet, but the shadow of Kangaroo Mountain. These lakes and meadows at the head of Hello Canyon would not see sunlight again until morning, but the sun still shone to the east of them. And to the west, on the far slope of Kangaroo. "As plain as night and day," we like to say, but night and day are not plain. Like microclimates, there are micronights—beside each boulder, behind each tree, on the east side of each mountain. And when the real night comes in, it does so stealthily. The prism of the earth's atmosphere, like any prism, bends light differentially, the blue more than the red. Alpenglow is red because the blue light has been bent out of it and is busy illuminating things down here in the shadows. This, too, will slowly fade as our point on the planet spins out of the penumbra and into the umbra. The light will become bluer and bluer, and at last disappear off the upper end of the visible spectrum. Night will have arrived. But where, in that process, is its edge?

Precisely the problem. Processes don't have edges. Processes have limits; but limits must not be confused with edges. Edges are definable, physical phenomena. Limits are definable only by their effects. And effects vary with the characteristics of what is being affected.

Which is possibly—no, it is probably—why we in the environmental community are having such a hard time conveying our anxiety about exploding populations and shrinking resource bases to the public at large. We are preaching limits; they are hearing edges. And edges are demonstrably not there. There is a limit to how many human beings the planet can support; there is a limit to how much oil we can extract, and how much iron we can mine, and how much timber we can sustainably cut. These limits are genuine, but like all limits they are fuzzy. We will know when they are here, but we will not be able to tell precisely when they arrive. There is too much confusion between the Ponderosas and the Jefferies, too much hemlock in isolated groves above the rest of the forest, too many people mistaking shadows for nightfall. It is only when we are all the way up, into the dark, starry night on the felsenmeer and the lichens and the snowbanks above the last knee-high, two-hundred-year-old, krummholzed whitebark pine that we will really know we are there. And that is all we will know. Not what is out there, nor where it started, nor how—or whether—we are going to get back out of it again. Only that it has arrived.

I sat up, and noticed that, for the first time since Hello Lake, the weasel did not sit up with me. A hopeful sign, though anything could still happen when I tried to stand and walk to the tent. The west peak of Red Buttes wore a sliver of orange light like a coronet; then that, too, was gone, and everything in the visible world was blue and dark. Becoming simultaneously bluer and darker, and who could unentwine those paired phenomena? On heavy, soft legs, with a heart that quivered but at least no longer fibrillated, I worked my way across the talus to the meadow and the waiting tent. Still at the limit, but back a bit from the edge. The spring near the tent was black in the darkness, findable more by sound and coolness than by sight. I dipped a cup into it and drank; then sat, waiting. Slowly, imperceptibly, the terminator whispered by. Then it was night.

III. The Left Hand of Eden

Thoreau's Doormat

When Henry David Thoreau went into the wood south of Concord to live the simple life surrounded by nature, the first thing he did was to log part of it. "I borrowed an axe," he tells us, "and went down to the woods by Walden Pond, nearest to where I intended to build my house, and began to cut down some tall arrowy white pines, still in their youth, for timber."

Thoreau does not record who the owner of the axe was, but it was probably Ralph Waldo Emerson. Walden Pond was not a howling wilderness, even in 1845; the pond lay less than twenty-five miles from the Boston waterfront and only about a mile from the center of Concord, and all the land around it was privately held. Thoreau had to work out a deal with the landholder whose property he wished to use before he could take up residence there. The landholder was Emerson. The "wildness" that the author of *Walden* so passionately defended as "the preservation of the world" was in fact a well-bounded and thoroughly subdued woodlot on which he was paying rent by keeping the thickets of blackberries under control.

All of which is a good deal less incongruous than it probably sounds. A house, in and of itself, does not separate one from nature; neither does dividing the landscape into meted and bounded, privately owned parcels, nor the management activity represented by clearing blackberries and tending the bean field Thoreau was so proud of, nor even the nearby hilltop "where the wood had been recently cut off," where the Hermit of Walden loved to stand and take in the view southward over the pond—a view that was possible only because logging had taken place there. Separation from nature is an attitude, not a condition. It is encouraged by houses and logging and property ownership, but it is not caused by these things. One can take part in them and still avoid it.

Thoreau managed. His snug little dwelling at Walden was weathertight, built of boards feathered out to their edges and overlapped, with shingles nailed on over those. Glass windows, uncurtained, let in the light; a fire crackled cheerily on a brick hearth at one end of the single room. The Fitchburg Railway ran close by, circling around the east end of the pond, and Thoreau often used its "yellow sand heap stretched away gleaming in the hazy atmosphere" as a road into town. Town was close by. It was just over a mile to Emerson's house, in which he had recently boarded and where he was still, throughout his stay in the "wilderness," regularly welcomed for supper.

But perhaps all this misses the point. The image of the foremost of our back-to-nature philosophers standing in a clearcut to admire the view, or strolling home along the railroad tracks from a convivial evening with friends toward a "wilderness" consisting of a piece of rented suburban real estate on which he has recently chopped down trees, cleared a field, and built a house, lacks incongruity for us because it lacks relevance. The defining fact of the Walden experiment was not Thoreau's house. It was Thoreau's doormat.

❦

Outside my own house just now it is raining—a cold November rain, drumming on the roof and pelting the few remaining leaves on the oak in the front yard. Snug behind glass, the furnace blowing and the cat sleeping in his basket at the head of the stairs, I watch the rain slant down from skies the color of stained pewter onto the sodden ground. The bird-feeder stands abandoned, the Steller's jays and juncos that were arguing over it a few minutes ago having fled to cover like the sensible creatures they are. The only person I see in the street is so thoroughly concealed beneath raincoat and umbrella that it is impossible to tell whether it is a man or a woman. I was out walking myself earlier, in the brief dry interval—perhaps an hour in length—between last night's rain and this morning's. It was a pleasant walk. But now I am grateful for the glass and the roof and the furnace.

There can be much positive about being outside in the rain. Scents are stronger then, and sweeter; the earth seems fresh and newly made. Views alternate between blurred and softened intimacy while the raindrops fly and stunningly etched detail are seen in the freshly washed intervals between squalls. The elemental pace of life seems to switch gears. One June a few years ago, my wife and I walked the south rim of our valley on the Pacific Crest Trail, from Siskiyou Summit on Interstate 5 to Greensprings Summit on Oregon Route 66. The distance is sixteen miles, and it took us two days. The rains began the first evening, shortly after we had set up our tent near the midpoint; they continued all that night and through most of the next day. With ponchos humped over our packs and flapping about our knees, we slogged along the muddy trail. Damp green meadows sloped upward into mist, bordered by conifers that we could barely see. Drops hung from the undersides of branches and lay in the cups of flowers like elfin wine. At intervals, holes would open in the clouds beneath us, offering windows to the valley and the distant town: the windows shifted gradually as we watched. Outcrops of lichen-covered basalt loomed along our path like dark buoys in the waves of the mountains. I have walked that stretch of trail since, in good weather. It was more comfortable, certainly; the views were bigger, the trail dryer, the resting spots considerably easier to use. But the magic had gone out of it. Of the two, it is the trip in the rain that I would most joyfully repeat.

All this is valid; but it is not the only valid position. The truth is that there is nothing whatsoever unnatural about wanting to get in out of the rain. The jays and juncos at my feeder proved that a few minutes ago; so does the cat in his basket, and the dog next door huddled under the protection of a tree, and the snake or rodent—it is difficult to tell which—whose burrow we recently spotted in the soft bank beneath the edge of the parking pad at the back of our lot. Humans are not the only animals that construct homes. There is nothing at all "natural" about discomfort.

Which brings us back to Thoreau's doormat. Thoreau knew the value of comfort, and the snug little house at Walden reflected this. The house was small, but not cramped: it measured twelve feet by fifteen feet, with an eight-foot ceiling. Sunlight falling through two big windows onto white plastered walls kept the place bright and airy, and there was the hearth for warmth. An attic and a cellar provided storage space for possessions and vegetables, respectively, and though his friend Ellery Channing made fun of their size—"by standing on a chair you could reach into the garret," Channing teased, "and a corn broom fathomed the depths of the cellar"—they were entirely adequate for Thoreau's purpose. Nor was the house devoid of furnishings. "None is so poor that he need sit on a pumpkin. That is shiftlessness," the poet wrote, and his room reflected this. It contained three chairs, a bed, both a table and a writing desk, and a variety of kitchen and personal implements. It did not contain a doormat. He tells us precisely why:

> *A lady once offered me a mat, but as I had no room*
> *to spare within the house, nor time to spare within*
> *or without to shake it, I declined it, preferring to*
> *wipe my feet on the sod before my door. It is best to*
> *avoid the beginnings of evil.*

That is the heart of Thoreau's message to us, right there. "It is best to avoid the beginnings of evil." And what is evil? Not comfort, but improvidence; not using nature to produce things you need, but using nature to produce things you don't need. Not possessing things, but allowing things to possess you. It was a code its author adhered to rigorously. Not even field samples picked up on his rambles about the Concord countryside were immune.

> *I had three pieces of limestone on my desk, but I was*
> *terrified to find that they required to be dusted daily,*
> *when the furniture of my mind was all undusted*
> *still, and I threw them out the window in disgust.*

Note that—as with the doormat—it is not really possession that is Thoreau's concern here, but upkeep. As long as the utility of an object exceeds its upkeep, its possession is defensible; but as soon as upkeep exceeds utility, open the window and heave the monster out. This holds for ideas as well as objects:

> *I left the woods for as good a reason as I went there.*
> *Perhaps it seemed to me that I had several more lives*
> *to live, and could not spare any more time for that*
> *one. It is remarkable how easily and insensibly we*
> *fall into a particular route, and make a beaten track*
> *for ourselves.*

The beaten track at Walden had become too clear, and too much time was being spent on maintaining it. The upkeep on the experiment had become higher than its utility. It was time to throw it out the window and move on.

As I write these words it is 150 years, less six months, since Thoreau picked up his borrowed axe and started chopping away at Emerson's pondside pines. That century and a half has seen the rise of a worldwide environmental movement that has sanctified the Hermit of Walden even as it has busied itself setting aside vast tracts of landscape on which to live as the Saint himself lived would be illegal. I do not wish to deny the utility of the wilderness concept; I value wilderness, use it, and have even done my share to promote it. But wilderness areas are possessions, and, as with all possessions, it is fair to ask where the accumulation of them should stop. How many pass the Thoreauvian test of utility versus upkeep? How many are chairs and tables and desks? How many are merely interesting pieces of limestone? How many are doormats?

Separation from nature is an extraordinarily hazardous attitude. There is severe danger in it. The "otherness" of the thing we have separated ourselves from is grounds for all kinds of mistreatment, from simple neglect through pillage, slaughter, and destruction. The presumed otherness of blacks, gays, Jews, aborigines, Christians—any group with at least one easily perceivable characteristic that happens to be noticeably different from the perceiver's own—has historically resulted in beatings, rapes, murders, lynchings, enslavement, and other outrages beyond number or description. The prevalent myth of American society, the frontier, has similarly created a sense of otherness between civilization and wilderness, a boundary beyond which codes of moral conduct no longer hold, and so we have raped and murdered and enslaved the wilderness. We who love nature have drawn lines around certain areas and said: *you cannot do this here*. But by the act of drawing the lines we have reinforced the otherness of these areas. We have taken a mythic beast called "wilderness" and locked it into a cage, and we should not be surprised to find the trophy hunters— whom we have now shown what the animal looks like— redoubling their efforts to hunt down those of its species still remaining in the wild.

We have locked development out of the wilderness. But by doing so, we have also unavoidably locked the wilderness out of development. This is not at all what we thought we were setting out to do.

Let me state this as clearly as I can: I am not in favor of the unrestricted development of our remaining wild areas. The idea of more clearcuts in the redwoods, or more strip mining in Appalachia, or more oversize homes with postage-stamp lawns swarming over the desert mountains of Arizona, is thoroughly abhorrent to me. Emotionally and philosophically I stand with the defenders of nature. I do not doubt the need for battle. What I have come to question—after many years of experience on the front lines—is our choice of weapons. We have put far too much trust in laws and boundaries and regulations. If you want to know how effective these are, reread your Thoreau. Start with the *Essay on Civil Disobedience*.

We have concentrated on changing behavior; what we really need to change are attitudes. We have mandated restrictions where we should be encouraging right conduct. We have attempted to teach the public, in maddening, unrelenting, and often self-conflicting detail, exactly what it is they may and may not do. What we really need to teach them is how to recognize doormats.

The laws of nature cannot be overruled, and that includes the laws of human nature. We need to understand all of them, take the whole range into account. Most of all, we need to be aware of the interactions among them. We are navigating across an unknown ocean beneath unfamiliar skies with no compass, no clock, and no calendar. It is hard work to study the stars and currents, hard to account for the vagaries of the winds and the changes of the seasons. Many may find it too hard. But it is the only sure way to set a course that will get us where we wish to go.

It has been three days since I began writing this essay. In that time the weather has changed dramatically. The storm I described earlier has passed, leaving our encircling mountains white with the winter's first significant snowfall. The air is lambent; the snow-covered trees on the distant ridges are pure white against pure blue, both colors so bright upon the eye that they make the eyelids ache. The sun fails to warm. The cat made one cautious foray into the bright but bitter yard and then retreated to the house. Now he is back in his basket at the head of the stairs, curled into bedding shaped to his own body, comfortable, familiar, and warm.

Animals are a lot like people.

People are a lot like animals.

Spotting the Owl

It was all very straightforward, really. They wanted to cut the trees down; we wanted the trees to stay up. They had tradition, profit, and most of the community on their side. We had a strong sense of moral outrage, coupled with enough science to make us pretty sure the cut would be seriously detrimental to most of the community in the long run. We had brought in a geologist from Montana to walk through the sale area to try to bolster our case. This was 1975, and few outside of a small cadre of cockeyed ornithologists had ever heard of an obscure speckled bird called the spotted owl.

The trees in question were California trees—northern California trees, so far north that a few of them had strayed over the border and were actually Oregon trees. They stood at the upper end of the Thompson Creek drainage, along the east side of the high ridge separating Thompson Creek from Indian Creek in the deep, green heart of the Siskiyou Mountains. Most were Douglas firs, but there were scatterings of true firs—Shasta reds, grands, nobles—and a few hemlocks and cedars. Occasionally, a pine. Big, craggy, thick-boled, they crowded the steep hillside like some dark enchantment, the sunlight filtering furtively through their crowns as if afraid to be caught touching the ground.

Sleeping beauty trees; Rumplestiltskin trees. Dogwood and maple grew beneath them.

Ten years before, there had been similar trees in the lower end of the Thompson Creek drainage. These were no longer there. In 1966, a wildfire of massive dimensions had swept through the area, blackening the slopes of Slater Peak and the south end of the Thompson Creek/Indian Creek divide; and what the fire had begun, the U.S. Forest Service had finished. Two years after the fire, in the name of "salvage," the lower Thompson Creek drainage had been stripped of all timber — black or green, it didn't matter—from the creek bed right up to the ridgeline. Nothing had grown back. In place of the fairy-tale forest there was now one huge clearcut, twenty square miles in area, bare of all but a few fireweed stems and blades of grass. Agency personnel had learned their lesson—they said. At Klamath National Forest headquarters in Yreka, sixty miles to the east, a picture of the Slater Peak clearcut was posted prominently on a wall above a caption that read, "This was our greatest mistake." The cut they had planned for upper Thompson Creek was much more modest: selective logging only, the forest canopy to be kept intact, ariel yarding methods—helicopters and high-lead cables—employed throughout in order to protect the soil. We still didn't trust them. We didn't think that any more of Thompson Creek should be logged at all.

So here we were, three of us—Diane Meyer, Bob Curry, and me—standing together at the edge of the ridgetop road that ran along the west side of upper Thompson Creek's big, green, soon-to-be-violated valley. Our plan was simple: drop off the ridge to the east, descend along Morgan Creek through the heart of the proposed timber sale to Thompson Creek itself, and walk out to the south, along the old, abandoned Thompson Creek Trail. Diane's husband Bill, who had just dropped us off, would pick us up someplace down in the Slater Peak clearcut that evening. A few tiny puffs of cloud highlighted an otherwise storybook-blue sky; the air-cooled rattle of the Meyers' well-used Volkswagen Microbus receded into an active silence of breeze and birdsong and faraway creek. It was 9:30 in the morning on a very beautiful June Saturday. We bent our heads over the map.

Diane was the current chair of the Pacific Northwest Chapter of the Sierra Club. A tall, athletic blonde in her early thirties, she was a botanist by training, with a master's degree in outdoor education from Southern Oregon State College on top of her undergraduate biology degree. Like many of us in the environmental movement of that time, her activism had been born in the antiwar protests of the sixties and thus carried with it an air of politics-as-moral-crusade which tended to unnerve opponents, especially when it came—as it usually did—coupled with a near-encylopedic grasp of their side of the issue as well as hers. This was not the first trip Diane and I had shared: she and Bill lived about a mile from my wife and me, and the four of us often hiked together. We had even co-led a couple of Sierra Club outings.

Bob was our Outside Expert. An associate professor of geology at the University of Montana in Missoula, he had a Ph.D. from Berkeley and a reputation for flamboyant but solid professional work in support of environmental causes. That—plus the fact that he had done a fair amount of field work in the hydrogeology of the California coast ranges— was what had caused us to contact him and offer to pay his way to southern Oregon. Stocky, muscular, and outgoing, he had a thick head of silvering curls and a puckish, goat-footed sense of humor that was quick to surface in conversation. It looked as though it might be hard to keep up with him once he was on the scent.

I was the counterweight. Nominally an "expert" as well—a reputation based on many hikes in the Siskiyous coupled with my position as chair of the Red Buttes Wilderness Council, the principal group opposing the Thompson Creek sale—I was painfully aware of my status as the only one present without formal scientific training. I knew nature, loved nature, had been immersed in nature since childhood. I was, in fact, making my living by writing about nature. But my education was in music. I normally relied on my biologist wife to keep my facts straight; here, I would have to rely on Diane and Bob. Despite the fact that both of them knew and accepted this, I felt apprehensive, not unlike the emperor just before the small boy pointed out that he was stark naked. Since the other two regularly did field work while I spent most of my time behind a desk, I thought they could probably out-hike me as well. Not good.

The map was on blueprint paper. Big, bulky, and difficult to fold and carry, it was nevertheless necessary for the work in front of us. It showed the sale area in photometrically derived detail on a scale of nearly a foot to the mile, with contour lines at ten-foot intervals. Sale units and soil units had both been blocked in. So—crucially—had all known landslides, both active and inactive. Those were what we had brought Bob in to look at. The soils of the Siskiyous are well-known for the widespread presence of what geologists term "mass instabilities," a characteristic which derives from the range's extraordinary geologic complexity. Mass instabilities have a tendency to become further unstable as timber is harvested from them. In other words, if you chop down the trees the landslides will slide. We had made loud complaints about this to the Forest Service, but they had been general complaints, complaints based on averages and hearsay. Once Bob had examined the ground directly beneath the proposed timber sale we would be able to be specific.

I raised my head from the map and looked around. The dirt surface of the road stretched north and south, crowded tightly on both sides by overhanging conifers. To the west the view was blocked by the top of the ridge, standing perhaps two dozen feet above us; eastward, the land dropped precipitously toward the creek, the near-clifflike nature of its descent disguised beneath its thick coat of fir. Small windows among the branches and trunks offered disconnected snapshots of the rocky row of peaks—Pyramid, Figurehead, Fourmile—along the opposite side of the valley. Snowfields streaked their summits.

In a few moments we would be headed down the steep, trailless slope beside us. *Where to?* I asked the question aloud, and Bob answered it. "There," he said, jabbing a thick finger at the map. I looked where the finger had come to rest: near Thompson Creek, on what the map indicated was the active face of the area's largest mass instability. The mass instability had a name. Neat LeRoy letters beside Bob's finger spelled it out: **Spotted Owl Slide.**

South Medford High School, Medford, Oregon, May 1, 1989. It is a warm weekday evening nearly fourteen years after Thompson Creek, and I am jammed into this forties-era high school auditorium with, it seems, half the population of southern Oregon. The auditorium has an official capacity of 940, but there are over 1000 of us packed into it. Twice that many are milling about outside. On the stage, in front of heavy red curtains, Jackson County's three county commissioners attempt, with little success, to keep order. Thirteen uniformed policemen—eleven from Medford plus two borrowed from nearby communities—stand against the wall, cocking their heads about like sparrows, looking for troublemakers. The room throbs.

Just days before, a federal judge in Seattle named William J. Dwyer had spoken, and the world turned upside down. Acting in a suit brought by several environmental groups against the Forest Service and the Bureau of Land Management, the judge had issued an injuction forbidding all further logging in the old-growth forests of the Pacific Northwest until the agencies had a plan in place to prevent the extinction of the various animal species dependent upon old growth for survival. All such animals were of concern, but the suit—and the judge—had specifically named only one: a large bird thought by biologists to be an "indicator species" for old growth. By this they meant that, if the bird's population was healthy, it could be reasonably assumed that the rest of the old-growth ecosystem was healthy as well. The bird was the spotted owl.

The moment the injunction was issued, the timber industry went ballistic. They called us "crazy enviros"; they called us much worse. The judge, and the environmental groups that had brought the suit, were guilty of "destroying the social fabric" of the Northwest. We "put owls before people"; we "ignored the welfare of the working man." Timber industry supporters were urged to tie yellow ribbons to the antennas of their cars, and overnight the streets of northwestern cities became the Yellow Sea. Here in Jackson County, the Board of Commissioners—stabbing vainly at the nonexistent middle in an attempt to head off what they termed "critical levels of confusion, hostility and fear in our community"—had drafted a resolution to Congress urging that the federal timber agencies be forced both to protect the owl *and* to produce the timber. The meeting at South Medford High School was billed as a hearing on that resolution. What it was turning into was a dogfight. There were no observers here; nothing but adamant partisans for one or the other of the opposing sides. About two-thirds of the crowd wore yellow, or had tied yellow ribbons through their buttonholes, but it was difficult to tell for sure what the timber beast/tree hugger split was because some of the yellow shirts were clearly decoys. I was wearing one myself. I had come to speak, and was carrying prepared testimony in my pocket; I hoped the shirt would get it listened to. Or at least keep me from being punched out. Neither of which, at the moment, looked anywhere near like a sure thing.

Speakers had been asked to indicate if they were going to testify as timber supporters or as environmentalists by signing up on separate lists, and the commissioners, in an attempt at evenhandedness, were lifting names from the two lists alternately. The crowd was rowdy and loud and full of barely corked violence. Once the cork very nearly came out. A name was called from the environmental list, and a frail-looking, middle-aged man in flannel shirt and suspenders, long hair and John Muir beard tinged with gray, limped slowly to the front of the room leaning on a cane. He identified himself to the microphone as "Bobcat." The nickname was evidently known; an angry murmur rustled through the yellow shirts, and two burly men in logging clothes surged to their feet and moved threateningly down the aisle. An older man in a business suit with a yellow ribbon in its lapel came to meet them as the police closed in. The business suit spoke to the logging clothes, quietly but urgently. The mob rumbled. The man called Bobcat turned to look out over the room, his gaze darting, intense. "*Are you afraid of me?*" he asked. The rumble swelled to near pandemonium. I thought: *Holy shit. We have awakened the beast that eats debate. The debate is dead. There is nothing left but the war.*

❦

It was dark and quiet under the trees. The going was trickier than it seemed; beyond the edge of the road there was little undergrowth, but the steep slope with its thick layer of loose duff made footing uncertain. Though one would not fall far here among all this vegetation, the swift slide and abrupt stop would be anything but comfortable. The three of us moved separately, each picking a slightly different path down the hillside. Fifty feet or so to my right, Diane seemed to be keeping her eyes primarily on the canopy. I suspected that this was illusory; experience told me that if any interesting plants showed up beside our feet, she would be the first to spot them. Off to the left, Bob was mostly invisible over the crown of the slope. When I caught sight of him, he was usually looking at the ground. Fine. That was what we were paying him for.

Because any trail is evidence that someone else has been there first, I love cross-country travel. It brings out the small boy in me, the one who devoured the journals of Lewis and Clark and wished fervently for a time machine. Given the choice, I prefer ridges with views, but the heart of a forest will do. In some ways it is better. The long lines of sight that ride the winds from open ridgetops are rarely able to sweep more than a few degrees around the horizon without encountering some jarring reminder of humanity: a road, a building, a clearcut; if nothing else, a vapor trail. In the trees, all such extraneous things are blotted out. The scene that greets your senses, the complex pattern of sights and sounds and scents that assails you, is one hundred percent natural. No artificial ingredients added.

It was the fashion once, among geographers, to refer to old-growth forests as "green deserts." This is crap. Old-growth forests are dense, teeming, wriggling masses of living things. Genetics has made us a forest-edge species, so we are more comfortable in that environment, and identify more with the plants and animals we find there. Because of this we think we see more of them. But the web of life is actually strung far thicker here.

Picking my way downslope, I found myself gradually tuning in to the hidden richness of the surroundings. At first, after the tangled riot of green at the road's edge, I noticed primarily the near-total absence of chlorophyll. There was green in the trees' needles, of course, but those were up in the canopy, sixty feet and more above me. Here at ground level the predominant colors were gray and brown. Dark gray on the trunks of the smaller trees, varying down the shades to deep brown—almost black—on the big ones. Rusty brown, the color of dead needles, on the ground, with a light gray undercoat—almost white—showing wherever the top layers of duff were scuffed up and the decomposed lower layers made visible. Dead colors. Until you noticed the life. Here, the wax-red of a saprophyte—broomrape, perhaps, or peppermint orchid—busily decomposing the dead roots of a tree. There, a flash of color from a flower— windflower, wood phlox, oxalis—leaves positioned precisely to take advantage of the momentary whispers of light from sunflecks moving to and fro across the forest floor. Broad leaves, so densely packed with chlorophyll that they were almost black. At the base of a pine stood a heap of cone fragments, the garbage dump of a rodent that had been feeding on the seeds at the base of the cone's scales. Nearby lay a short, twisted rope of fur and broken bone—the remains of a small mammal, perhaps the same rodent that had created the scale heap. An owl had caught it, digested the good parts, and, in the standard manner of its kind, regurgitated the rest.

The wind, too, had been at work. Here and there were standing snags, dead trees with their tops snapped off. Some were of immense size. Most were riddled with neat, rectangular holes several inches tall and a couple of inches wide. Pileated woodpeckers looking for grubs had made those. The tops, and some whole trees, lay on the ground where they had fallen; the downed trees' root wads waved in the air above shallow cavities in the soil. A few of the jackstrawed tree trunks were fresh, their broken ends still oozing sap. The others varied from old to ancient; in some cases they could be located only by inference as you observed the straight lines of sturdy, middle-aged offspring they had nursed to life along their decaying backbones. There is no law mandating curbside pickup in an old-growth forest, but the trees recycle anyway. They always have.

In fact, it is recycling that most completely characterizes this ecosystem—recycling, and the complex interdependencies among plants and animals that the recycling fosters. Back at the road, it was very much every plant for itself; trees, shrubs, herbs, all competing for space, jostling and crowding each other, each one perfectly willing to strangle its neighbor for a few more square inches of sunlight. Here in the deep woods the norm was cooperation. Plants and animals, predators and prey, parasites, saprophytes and chlorophytes—all fit into a tight, circular scheme in which each tiny piece was important. Consider, for example, that owl pellet back there. I was not enough of a zoologist to be able to identify the remains of the creature that the owl had eaten, but one common owl prey species in old-growth is the red tree vole, and this might easily have been one of those. If so, I was looking at a crucial cog in the machine that keeps the old-growth forest alive. The red tree vole, an elusive creature closely related to the common meadow mouse, has developed an evolutionary craving for the fruiting bodies of mycorrhizal fungi. Mycorrhizal fungi are truffles—underground mushrooms—which have built a symbiotic relationship with the roots of green plants. The fungi penetrate the roots with tiny strands of protoplasm called hyphae; they send other hyphae ranging out into the soil. From the host plant they obtain sugars and other complex carbohydrates. From the soil they obtain water-soluble elements, particularly phosphorous, a share of which they pass on to the plant. Without each other, both the fungi and the plants would die of malnutrition. And without the red tree vole, old-growth conifers would be without the fungi. Because the truffles that are their fruiting bodies lie completely under the earth, their spores cannot be carried about by the wind. In order to spread to new ground, they need to eaten by the voles. The digestion-resistant spores pass through the voles and are deposited wherever the voles defecate, and that is where the baby fungi grow.

But without owls, there would be no red tree voles. Without predation, vole fecundity would be so high that the species' survival would be jeopardized. This is only partly because they would overshoot their food supply: mostly, it is simple mathematics. The equations that govern population growth in living things, we now know, embody a form of strange attractor—one of those odd mathematical objects that generate chaotic patterns in time within predictable patterns in space. The type of attractor involved is called a "logistical hump," and its form is tightly dependent on the variable that, in the population equations, represents fecundity. At low values of this variable, the attractor is a single rising line. Push it higher, and the line becomes bimodal, separating into two distinct alternating nodes. Push it higher yet, and it goes chaotic. Succeeding runs which differ only slightly in fecundity will show wildly varying patterns of actual reproductive success, some extremely high, others approaching zero. No species can survive very long with a reproductive scattering like that. And the fecundity of voles is so high that, even at full levels of predation, vole populations are already in the bimodal stage. Take the predation away, and you drive them very quickly into chaos. Which means extinction. The voles disappear; the mycorrhiza stop spreading; the trees get sick. The whole ecosystem goes into massive disarray. All because a few owls have stopped eating a few voles.

I caught up with Bob. He was standing at the base of an immense Douglas fir, eight feet through and well over 100 feet tall. The heavy, curved bole of the trunk leaned into the mountainside at an angle of around fifteen degrees. It looked precariously close to going over. The geologist gestured. "Mass wastage," he said triumphantly. "Look around. They're all doing that." Indeed, all the trees in the vicinity were tipped into the slope; most less so than the tree Bob stood beneath, but all easily noticeable once they were called to your attention. Slow creep of the soil down the mountain was doing that, pulling the butts of the trees out from under their crowns. Sixty feet or so upslope the duff abruptly stairstepped about six inches. Headscarp. We had reached the top of the slide.

8:30 p.m. During a break between witnesses, the commissioners announced that the hearing would recess at 8:45; when it took up again at 9:00, it would be with a new audience, an audience composed of those currently milling about outside the building. In that way, they pointed out, twice as many people as the auditorium actually held would be able to attend. Meanwhile, in those last fifteen minutes of the first group's portion of the proceedings, four more people would be allowed to testify. Their names were announced. Mine was not among them. A disappointment, but also a relief. I took the typed notes for my three-minute speech from my pocket and began smoothing out the creases, preparing them to be turned in, at the break, as written testimony.

The most riveting moment of the hearing—possibly excepting the near-mugging of Bobcat—had come only a few minutes before. A tall, slightly stooped young man in a sports jacket and tie had approached the microphone. His name was Gary Schrodt. "I am a wood-products manufacturer," he began, "who is in favor of protecting the spotted owl." Hecklers on both sides paused, attempting to sort this out. For the first time all evening the room fell silent.

If Schrodt was aware of the impact of his opening statement, he didn't show it. He spoke into the silence, ignoring the house, looking straight at the commissioners. He was, he said, the owner of a secondary wood products firm, a company that made redwood bird houses out of wastes it purchased from lumber mills along the California coast. He considered himself a preservationist; he wanted to see as much old growth as possible left standing. The key was more efficient utilization of the timber we had. Secondary wood products were the wave of the future. Currently, the timber industry utilized less than 60 per cent of the volume of each tree it took from the woods; recovery of even half that waste would mean we could have a wood products industry the same size as today's on twenty per cent less harvest. "I work hard for my living, and I depend on timber for my livelihood," he concluded. "There's room for both owls and people. We must support both." He returned to his seat. There was—perhaps predictably—little applause. In a room full of deeply divided partisans, Schrodt had dared to stand with the commissioners in the middle, and he was not going to be rewarded for it. Even though he was undoubtedly right.

The last speaker was winding down. Something about how humans were more important than owls, and how her little girl (cute kid, with a yellow ribbon in her hair) wouldn't have enough to eat if the timber industry was kept out of the old growth. The commissioners conferred briefly among themselves. Commissioner Jeff Golden stepped forward. He asked us to leave the auditorium by the front exits: that way, the crowd outside could come in the back at the same time and refill the room. Those of us who hadn't had a chance to deliver our testimony could leave it, if we wished, in a box at the edge of the stage. We all stood, and I allowed myself to be carried by the crush of the crowd to the front of the room, where I worked upstream along the apron of the stage to the box that Commissioner Golden had indicated. This must be how a salmon feels in a waterfall. Literally pulling myself along the apron, I managed to deposit my eggs in the redd and, energy spent, abandoned myself to the downstream flow. We poured out the jammed doorway and into the liberating night.

In the dark a short distance outside the door I spotted a familiar face: Diane Meyer. She was deep in conversation with a man wearing a vest festooned with at least six yellow ribbons. Odd, I thought, until I noticed that the man was Ed Kupillas. Ed was an executive with one of the biggest of southern Oregon's timber companies, and he and I were often called on to debate one another; as a result of that contact, and despite our differences, we had found ourselves becoming friends. A thoughtful and articulate man, he took a hard-line stance in public but softened it in private. I suspected he had helped to write the resolution that the county commissioners were taking testimony on tonight. Though that suspicion would later prove wrong, there was good reason for it at the time. One of the commissioners was suspected to be leaning heavily toward the industry side of the debate; another was known to lean just as heavily toward the preservationists. The third commissioner—the one holding firmly to the middle ground, the place where the resolution had come down—was Ed's wife.

He glanced at my yellow shirt as I strolled up. "Which side are you on?" he asked.

"Shhh," I stage-whispered, glancing from side to side. "I'm incognito."

He smiled. "You have a yellow ribbon on your car antenna?"

"I haven't gone quite that far."

"I've got both yellow and green on mine," said Diane. "Keeps 'em guessing."

"Means you can get shot at by either side." Ed jabbed a thumb over his shoulder at the auditorium. "What did you think?"

"It's crazy," I said. "All emotion, no reason."

Diane leaned forward. "For a moment there, I really thought Bobcat was going to get himself beat up."

Ed smiled. "Some of the boys are a little hot under the collar," he said. "You can't blame them. They're worried about their jobs."

"Which are dead anyway at the rate you guys are cutting."

"And shouldn't be the issue, anyway," I interjected. "The issue should be the health of the forests. If they go, all of us lose."

Ed nodded. "I have argued very forcefully in the councils of the industry," he said, "that we are making a mistake by leaning so hard on the jobs issue. I think it's going to come back to haunt us." He gestured impatiently. "Everybody knows that employment in this industry goes up and down in cycles that depend on housing starts. We can't guarantee a job to anyone, and we're creating false expectations that we can. The next time we have to lay off people because of the economy, labor is going to come down all over us."

"With reason."

"With good reason. We're setting ourselves up. We need to get off jobs and start talking about access to the resource."

"Loggers are an old-growth-dependent species," I said. "They just don't recognize it. But when the old growth goes, they're going to go with it, at least in the form most of them in there recognize."

"We're not fully old-growth dependent," Ed protested. "We can live on second growth. What's really hurting us is the uncertainty. We can't plan. If we were guaranteed a land base to work with, we'd know how much timber we could plan for. As it is, the only thing we can do is keep trying to grab as much as possible. Just like you guys."

"Longer rotations might be the key." I was referring to the cycle of harvest, planting, growth, and harvest again that takes place in managed forests. If those cycles were long enough, I was thinking, the second-growth forests would have time to take on old-growth characteristics. Then the argument over how much old growth we needed to preserve would become moot.

"We could live with long rotations if the land base was guaranteed," Ed agreed. "The important thing is certainty."

"How about 200 years?"

He hesitated only slightly. "We could live with that."

"Everybody could probably live with that," said Diane, "But no one would think they could."

The tall figure of Gary Schrodt emerged out of the darkness. "I could live with that," he said.

Ed looked at him. "If you're going to testify at these things," he said, "you're going to have to learn to stop making sense."

❧

We found the Meyers' Microbus about 7:00 p.m. Long light stroked the grasses in the Slater Peak clearcut and yellowed the forests we had come from, further up the canyon. The shadow of the Microbus reached far down the hill. Bill Meyer was nowhere around. There was a note: he was hiking down by the stream. He would be watching the road if we decided to start driving out. Diane thought we probably should. It was better than a two-hour drive back to Ashland; even starting now, it would be after 9:00 by the time we got home. But Diane was just starting to work on her drivers' license, and this was a terrible place to practice. If the car was going anywhere, the driver would have to be Bob or me.

"I have one of these," said Bob, referring to the Microbus. "I can drive." He didn't look totally convinced. Actually, he looked ill. All the way up through the clearcut he had walked like a man forcing himself to move; like someone who, having already exerted himself too much, was now paying for it with a throbbing headache and nausea. Which, he admitted, he was.

"That's OK," I assured him. "I have one of these, too." I got behind the wheel, pulled the keys down from the visor where Bill had left them, and prepared to start the engine, fully satisfied with the day. We had done exactly what we set out to do: we had traversed the Thompson Creek sale from top to bottom, right down over the Spotted Owl Slide. Bob had a notebook full of observations on the state and stability of the earth beneath the trees; I had another day in the deep woods, and a look at Thompson Creek before it was logged. Which it would be, despite our appeal and Bob's impassioned testimony, two years later.

Two moments in particular stood out. The first was our conversation during lunch, someplace along Morgan Creek. The creek was narrow—perhaps eighteen inches wide—and chock full of woody debris, branches and whole logs lying across it and in it. The creek pooled behind the debris and ran over it, descending the mountain in a series of small waterfalls. The V of exposed earth formed by its banks looked raw and unsightly. Trees crowded close to the edge, ready to tumble over and join those already in the creek. Munching on a sandwich, Bob gazed at the chaotic scene. "That," he observed, "is one of the healthiest watercourses I have ever seen."

He explained. On a steep slope like this, on such unstable soils, one would normally expect a creek this size to be much more deeply incised—probably all the way to bedrock. Whole, broad hunks of the mountainside should be peeling off. That wasn't happening. The reason was the woody debris. Lying there in the creekbed, it formed a series of natural check dams, slowing the flow of the water—thus reducing its erosive power—and allowing the soil carried in the water to settle out. The trees along the upper rim of the creek's V also helped; their roots were stabilizing the banks, so the creek couldn't erode them as rapidly. And when they were finally undermined and fell in, they simply made more check dams. "That's what the forest means to this slope," said Bob. "Stability. Complex geologic structures like this are highly unstable. But if you increase the complexity by adding life, you actually reduce the instability. The more complex, the more stable. Any growth will help, but an old, highly developed forest like this is best. That's why I fight timber sales."

That was the first moment. The second came as, working down through the trees, I finally caught sight of Thompson Creek itself. Thompson Creek was big, more river than creek: twenty or thirty feet wide, three or four feet deep, it came surging down its valley, swinging around boulders, pouring over logs, foam-flecked and exuberant in the sunlight. Though we would find bits and pieces later, there was at first no sign of the abandoned trail. This was the wildest, most remote, most *uncivilized* large stream I had ever seen. After all those years, I thought I might at last be glimpsing some small particle of what Lewis and Clark had found in their protean journey to the Western Ocean. Even a trail can ruin a wilderness. There was, in fact, I suddenly realized with overwhelming clarity, little difference at all between a trail and the Slater Peak clearcut, except size.

Time to leave. I had my hand on the key; Diane was getting into the back. Suddenly she stopped, one foot on the floor of the bus, the other still on the ground. "Listen," she said.

I had already caught it: a faint, distant call, yaps rising to contrapuntal howls, hanging in the air more like images than sounds; a shape of decibels; a wild architecture of animal music. Coyote?

Diane shook her head. "I don't think so. Might be, but it sounds like it's coming from the forest. A coyote would be likely to be out here in the open. I think it's a spotted owl. The males sometimes call to the females that way. Shhh—she might answer."

The three of us sat quietly. A moment, two; and then a distant whistle, much more birdlike, faint to us, but sounding like it would rip your ears out up close; a clear note, rising to a shriek of angry joy that stopped suddenly. A repeat of the first call, the second joining it, soaring over it like a high *cantus*. Pause. The whistling call, alone once more. An amber silence into which the sound of winds and distant water gradually returned.

"I'll be damned," said Bob.

What I was going to say to the hearing was this: We are all old-growth-dependent species. We wear a civilization which we change like dress with the fashion, but the body beneath remains the same, and the body lives on the earth. Maintaining the machinery of nature is no less important to us than maintaining our homes and vehicles, and for the same reason: without care, the machinery wears out. Use it, but preserve it. The gulf between the sides is a false dichotomy. If you don't preserve it, you can't use it. If you don't use it, there is no point in preserving it.

But you cannot preserve it by creating preserves, any more than you can use it by using it up. Old growth is not a place, it is a condition. It is a complex of simple things, stable because of both the simplicity and the complexity. It is spotted owls, yes, but it is also trees and earthworms and woody debris in the streams and the children of loggers playing beside a freshly cut stump. It is the continuing process of the planet that keeps us alive. The calls of owls and children are the sound of the earth's breathing. They are the assurance that there is, after all, a future.

We can have enough timber, and we can have enough wilderness, but only if we are willing to alter our sense of what both "timber" and "wilderness" mean. Technically, the answer is probably the very long rotations that Ed and Diane and Gary and I spoke of. Politically, it lies in seeking the true balance of consensus rather than the false center of compromise, in finding ways to make certain that all voices in the debate are not only heard, but own a piece of the solution. Spiritually, it is both much simpler than these things, and much harder. Spiritually, the answer lies in acceptance of the idea that the word *dependence* means exactly what it says: *reliance for support on something other than ourselves*. Not to make it over in our image, but to allow it to remain Other. Neither a green cathedral nor a tree farm, but a set of coherent creatures and places and processes that own themselves, a complex and interdependent structure into which we, too, despite our protests, fit. A fabric. A forest. Life.

A short distance down the road we spotted Bill Meyer, silhouetted against the valley, swinging up through the long blue light of the hillside shadows on a path that would intersect the car. I turned the wheel over to him and sank gratefully into the front passenger seat as he drove us, in his wood-paneled vehicle, away from the trees whose preservation would kill the timber industry, through the clearcut whose relentless repetition would kill it just as dead. We headed for the highway. Night was beginning to fall.

A short distance from the auditorium I passed a group of protesters with pro-timber placards headed, as I was, toward the cars. Two families with kids, clean-cut and smiling. Nice people. Engaged in a violent, useless fight with other nice people in which both sides were going to have to lose. Either that, or both were going to have to win. I sank gratefully into the driver's seat and headed for the freeway. Night had already fallen, but the next event in the cycle, after the night, is always the sunrise.

The Left Hand of Eden

Who killed Cock Robin?

— old English folk song

Other than a few strategically placed puffs of cumulus, the sky above the slowly moving car is a deep, achingly pure blue. The road curves upward along a mountainside so close to perpendicular that when we look to the right, most of what we see is the growing tips of large, downslope conifers. To the left, embankment; ahead, coarse gravel scattered over steep roadbed. The smells drifting through the open windows are of a world that has not yet cast off morning.

Our goal this perfect early-August day is Hershberger Mountain, a steep-sided andesite plug thrust upward from subalpine meadows near the upper end of the Rogue-Umpqua Divide in southern Oregon's share of the Cascade Mountains. The plug has a fire lookout perched near its summit, and the lookout and this road to it are what kept Hershberger out of the Rogue-Umpqua Divide Wilderness when it was created by Congress in 1984. The crest of the slope to our left forms the wilderness boundary; when the road gains the crest, a few miles further along, its edge and the wilderness edge will coincide precisely for a mile or so. For me this will be a moment of distinctly mixed feelings.

As an environmental activist in Oregon during the seventies and early eighties, I helped midwife the Rogue-Umpqua Divide Wilderness into being. But I have since come to believe that the wilderness-preservation concept is deeply flawed, and that the Wilderness Act itself—well intentioned and forward-looking as it was—has destroyed more wilderness, here and elsewhere, than it will ever have a chance to save.

A heretical thought, which I shall suppress for the moment. It is a spectacularly beautiful day. We are going flower-rambling.

The Rogue-Umpqua is part of what geologists refer to as the Western Cascades Province. Its rocky vertebrae were laid down in the Miocene epoch, about twenty-five million years ago. Like the more famous High Cascades a few miles to the east, the Western Cascades are chiefly volcanic in origin; but the volcanoes here are long dead, and most have worn down to the hard stone of their hearts. Long, steep-sided ridges finger among flat-floored, green valleys. Mixed conifers, primarily Douglas fir and western hemlock, floor the valleys and spill up their slopes; near the tops of the ridges, at an elevation of around 6,000 feet, true firs and mountain hemlocks take over, and there are broad reaches of flower-filled subalpine meadow. From these ridges the rocky cores of the ancient volcanoes rise like weathered battlements. It is not a spectacular landscape, but for sheer loveliness one would be hard-pressed to find its equal. A Victorian visitor, one O. C. Brown, thought it "the grandest summer resort in Oregon," and though the crowds have gone elsewhere—or perhaps, in part, *because* the crowds have gone elsewhere—that statement still seems true today. "The juxtaposition of rocky outcroppings, dense forest and gentle meadow is magical," enthused naturalist Art Bernstein after a 1987 visit to Hershberger. "The only place I've ever seen a greater concentration of wildflowers was at Paradise Park on Mt. Rainier."

We are a little after the peak of flower season, but I would not want to dispute Bernstein's judgment. Approaching the ridge, the car seems to glide hub-deep through red paintbrush and white and yellow umbrelliferae. Phalanxes of asters float among the grasses like lavender mists. Ahead, the lookout looms on its cone of rock like a postcard view of a Rhine castle.

Just at the base of the summit pyramid the road meets the wilderness boundary and swings left, across the ridge. The boundary swings with it. We traverse the west side of the mountain, dropping gently through a steep, damp meadow of grasses and rock outcrops and little springs bright with yellow and red monkey flowers. Soon the road bears right again, climbing briefly to a saddle filled with noble fir and mountain hemlock. Here it doubles sharply back to begin the final steep climb to the lookout. A half-mile of cobble-dodging in low gear and we are there, on a ragged, forty-foot-wide platform blasted out of the gray andesite; north of us and fifty feet further up, the lookout; east, west, and south a brow of smooth, hard rock and, beyond it, the spherical immensity of mountain space. Lines of red paintbrush bob in the breeze above crevices that appear too small to hold their sustaining soil.

I brake the car to a halt and we run to the view, across the gravel platform and out onto the elemental rock. We seem to be bathing in sunlight and scenery. Fifteen miles to the east, across the upper Rogue River Basin, the raw rim of Crater Lake—part of the High Cascades—looms another 1,500 feet above us. Westward in no particular order the tumbled ridges of the Western Cascades fade toward the invisible Pacific. South and west the line of sight is longest. Nearly forty miles off in that direction, tiny but sharply defined through the lambently clear air, we can make out the distinctive truncated-pyramid shape of Mount Ashland. That is out of the Cascades altogether. Mount Ashland and its neighbors are part of the Siskiyou Mountains, a subrange of the Klamaths—a rugged and little-known mountain system that was ancient before any part of the Cascades had raised its steaming head above the vast but shallow waters of the Miocene Intracratonic Sea.

Much closer at hand—four hundred feet below us and wrapping our parapet on three sides—are the meadows we drove through a few minutes ago on our way up here. From this distance the flowers disappear into the grasses and the meadows glow a lush, emerald green, set off by darker greens in the ragged border of mountain hemlock. Most of the meadow system lies to the east of the road and thus, though it is by far the most attractive feature of the vicinity, it is outside the wilderness and unprotected. There was a time— not too many years ago—when I would have considered this *prima facie* evidence that the Rogue-Umpqua Divide Wilderness was too small, and that I should therefore work toward closing the road and expanding the wilderness boundary. I see things a bit differently now. The boundary does not lie where it does because the efforts of environmentalists were a failure. It lies where it does because the Wilderness Act itself is a failure.

I have stated this elsewhere many times; let me state it again here. I am not in favor of the further destruction of wildlands. I am no friend of development. Whenever I think of the "invisible hand" of Adam Smith, the pose my mind's eye gives it is the familiar one with the back of the hand toward us and the middle finger pointed straight up in the air. The idea that this landscape—these views, these trees and meadows, this stone, this air—should be ground up and fed into the maw of "progress," to be digested messily for a while and then deposited in a smelly heap where the beast crouches for a moment behind a bush, is thoroughly abhorrent to me.

But in our haste to halt this dire scenario, we in the environmental movement have rushed into battle wielding the wrong weapons. We have countered the developers' visions of Eden with visions of an Eden of our own: an untouched, pristine planet against an endless cornucopia of consumer delights. But while the right hands of these Edens beckon sensuously, the left hands—ours as well as theirs— rend and destroy. What is needed, here at the close of the twentieth century as the human species threatens to overwhelm the planet, is not conflicting Edens: what is needed is a healthy dose of reality.

I turn and look north. In that direction there is still mountain in the way, rock and meadow and stunted conifers rising to a point two hundred feet above us and a third of a mile distant. It is lovely, but it blocks the view. This makes the fire lookout here less than one hundred per cent effective. More to the point, given the current line of thought, it keeps us from seeing Rattlesnake Mountain, five miles to the north. Another andesite plug, similiar in many respects to Hershberger, Rattlesnake nevertheless differs in one important way: it is entirely within the Rogue-Umpqua Divide Wilderness. And if there is any place on the planet which should be cited as the source of my current discontent with the methods and techniques of the modern environmental movement, Rattlesnake Mountain is that place.

❦

When telling a tale, it is usually best to follow the advice the King of Hearts gave to the White Rabbit: *begin at the beginning and procede until you come to the end. Then stop.* The beginning you seek, however, may be conceptual rather than chronological. To tell the tale of what I have since come to call the Rattlesnake Epiphany it seems necessary to start, not on Rattlesnake, but a year later and a continent away, midway through the long journey—three months, twenty thousand miles—that I took to test the epiphany's truth.

The first of the three episodes I wish to relate here took place in downtown New Haven, Connecticut, on a warm Wednesday morning in early September, 1992. My wife, Melody—the other half of the "us" I keep referring to here on Hershberger—had accompanied me through the first half of my journey, but her schedule is tied to the academic year at Southern Oregon University and it was time for her to go home. The means she had chosen for this, several months before while we were still in the planning stage, was by Amtrak from New Haven. So we had found the train station, and confirmed her reservation and checked her bag through, and we had a couple of hours to kill—and lunch to buy—before the train left.

One of the discoveries we have made while traveling together is the advantage of mall food courts for quick meals in strange towns. Granted, what you get is primarily fast food, but there is usually a wide variety of fast food, generally in a clean, attractive setting, and when one of you has an appetite that tends toward Chinese while the other dotes on baked potatoes and burgers, finding a mall is usually the surest way to satisfy both. So we asked the ticket agent about the locations of the local malls. He recommended one called Chapel Square, about six blocks away. Comfortably close. We decided to leave the car in the parking garage at the train station and walk.

Walking in downtown New Haven—I'm sure most New Haven residents will agree with me—is not a pleasant experience. The place is dull, worn, dingy. Like most American cities it was long ago given over to the automobile, and the result is not just a continual stream of traffic, but a continual miasma of exhaust, settling uniformly over the buildings, the sidewalks, and the souls of the passers-by. You hear motors; you see thick air and old, tired buildings, dirty in appearance no matter how thoroughly they may be scrubbed. You cannot escape the constant desire to look furtively over your shoulder. In six blocks it can wear deeply on you. We were happy and relieved when we finally located the mall entrance.

Happy and relieved, but a bit puzzled. Though it was clearly labeled "Chapel Square Mall," what we appeared to have found was just a mid-block storefront in a nondescript building, no different from other storefronts and buildings we had passed between there and the train station. Still, it had the right name and it was in the right location. We pushed inside, past the security guard and the metal detector (I remember a metal detector, though I may be imagining it) . . .

. . . and found ourselves in a large, suburban-style, two-story mall, flooded with light and bright with white paint. It was end-on to the street, and it stretched some distance away from us. We walked on, a bit dazed, beneath the big skylights, past the open storefronts and the benches and the greenery—typical mall scenery, but wildly out of sync with what was just outside the door. At the far end of the second floor was the food court. The Chinese-food lover and I chose our separate poisons and met at a table by the back wall. The back wall was glass. On the far side, clean and green and bathed—it seemed—in a much purer and more elemental sunlight, were the lawns and trees and neat brick buildings of Yale University.

The second episode in my group of three actually happened nearly a month before New Haven: August 7, 1992, in Great Smoky Mountains National Park. We drove into the park from the north, through Gatlinburg, Tennessee, morose and mountain-hungry after two flat weeks on the Great Plains and a couple of hilly days in Kentucky. It quickly became apparent that the Smokies were not going to disappoint us. The great green walls of LeConte Mountain and the Chimney Tops loomed over the valley of the Little Pigeon as we climbed toward Newfound Gap, at 5,048 feet higher than all but a handful of passes at home in Oregon. The valley narrowed; the Little Pigeon foamed and sang over boulders beside us. Several times we stopped to take advantage of a Great Smoky Mountains National Park innovation called Quiet Walks—trails in the woods which go to no place in particular, but which serve to get you off the road and into a natural setting for a little while. The parking lots for the Quiet Walks are small, to insure that walkers will not be disrupted by hordes of their fellow humans. Because there are plenty of Quiet Walks, and because the trails go to no specific scenic overlooks, the system works. If the parking lot for one Walk is full, there is no sense of loss whatever in going on and trying for the next.

From Newfound Gap itself, at what is very nearly the geographic center of this large park, a spur road heads west, climbing even higher along the crest of the Smokies toward Clingman's Dome. We turned onto it. Clouds wreathed the summits; there would be no views. But Clingman's Dome rises higher than any other point in the park—higher, in fact, than any other point east of the Mississippi save one, North Carolina's Mt. Mitchell, a few miles northeast of the park boundary—and even here, south of a large part of

Tennessee, this would mean rock outcrops and subalpine flowers and stunted conifers, the things we missed most from back home.

The Clingman's Dome road ended a few hundred yards below the summit, in the clouds. We hiked the trail toward the top through damp, blowing fog, wrapped in parkas, getting wet and cold anyway. The rocks were there all right, and the flowers, and the longed-for sights and scents of the high mountains. But what we found ourselves noticing most were the dead trees.

The upper reaches of the Smokies are the home of the Fraser fir, a small-needled subalpine species closely related to the balsam fir of the far north. Their presence here, a bit of the North Woods more than a thousand miles south of Hudson Bay, is one of the main contributors toward the park's special, otherworldly character. But over ninety-five percent of the mature Fraser firs in the park are now dead. The park has protected them from lumbermen and suburban sprawl; it has not protected them, and cannot protect them, from the twin traumas of smog and exotic insects, neither of which pay any attention to human-drawn boundaries. Approximately seventy percent of the Smokies' famous smoke is now smog, which weakens trees' immune systems in much the same way as it weakens ours. The weakened firs are no match for the wooly adelgid, a European beetle which was introduced accidentally to Maine around the beginning of the twentieth century and has been working its way south ever since. In another decade, the white carcasses that commanded our attention on Clingman's Dome are likely to be all that is left to remind us that there was once something wild in this world called a Fraser fir. There will be tamed and tended Frasers on Christmas-tree farms; that is something. But it is hardly the same.

The last of my three tales requires a little background explanation, plus an affirmation that it is all true. The other two tales have been true, as well; but what I am about to say sounds so bizarre that it seems necessary to reassure you, here at the outset, of its absolute veracity.

In the spring of 1981, in the midst of field research for my 1982 book *Nor Any Drop to Drink*, I came to Louisville, Kentucky to look at a place called Valley of the Drums. Stumbled across by reporters and environmental workers in late 1979, the valley was the largest known illegal waste dump in the country and, with Love Canal, one of the two chief reasons for passage of the Superfund law the next year. I had contacted my brother, Jack, a music professor at the University of Louisville, and he had done the local footwork for me, including setting up a tour to be guided by Jim Detjen of the Louisville *Courier-Journal*—one of the reporters who had blown the lid off the place fourteen months before. The three of us drove out to the valley on an overcast morning in late March. Here is part of my description of that visit, as it appeared in *Nor Any Drop to Drink*:

> *Jim led the way down the path; Jack and I gingerly followed. For an hour the three of us prowled among drums. Red drums, green drums, yellow drums, blue drums. Drums relatively intact, stacked in long neat rows. Drums thick with corrosion standing in the center of spreading stains. Drums cascading down hillsides like lethal Niagaras; drums humping into rusting and grotesque caricatures of the surrounding hills. Drums everywhere. The sick-sweet smell of solvents hung in the air so heavily that its odor could almost be seen.*

In September 1992, a few days after putting Melody on the train in New Haven, I found myself once more in Louisville and decided to go for another look at the Valley. The place had reportedly been pretty well cleaned up, and the Environmental Protection Agency was no longer actively working on it, but they still owned the land. "I understand there's a locked gate across the driveway," Jack told me. "You may not be able to get in." He went off to teach his classes; I located the place on map and in memory and headed out. Found it easily, clean as a whistle, just as reported. And the locked gate was there, too. But there was no fence. The chain-link gate with its massive padlock stood alone athwart the drive like a foolish little copy of the Arc de Triomphe. You could—and I did—walk all the way around it, running camcorder in hand to record the feat.

Atop Hershberger Mountain the view south still draws, but the pull of the flowers has begun to feel stronger. We stop at the car long enough to grab our fanny packs, my walking staff, and the knapsack containing lunch, and then head north toward the mountain's true summit, a third of a mile away. The first twenty feet lie up the face of a large andesite outcrop, surmounted by a steep steel stairway; then trail takes over, winding north to a small saddle and doubling back to the open knoll holding the lookout. The lookout is unmanned. We return to the saddle and leave the trail, following faint paths north. The ridge is all natural rock garden, meadow and stone and stunted trees arranged with a harmony that human design could not possibly achieve. Art Bernstein was right: the effect is magical. We climb slowly, savoring.

I think what I have been trying to tell you with my three tales is this: at least as it is currently practiced, legislated environmental protection is a fraud. It is a failure not only practically, but conceptually. Nearly all of it involves borders in some manner. And borders are a human phenomenon, not a natural one. Their effect, when they work at all, is to confer special status on the areas within them, something which can only be done at the expense of the world outside. Yale and the Chapel Square Mall separate themselves from the rest of downtown New Haven, which declines as a result—a decline that is easier to ignore because one can always take refuge from it in the university and the mall. Our parks and wilderness areas operate in much the same way. They don't preserve nature: all they preserve is the illusion that we are doing something. And that makes it easier to justify destruction elsewhere. We're tearing the hell out of the landscape, but we've got all these little bits protected, and ultimately everything is going to be all right.

But ultimately everything isn't. It isn't, because human boundaries are totally transparent to natural forces. The winds cross them, bringing the smog; the woolly adelgid arrives, and the trees die. All we have done in the name of environmental protection turns out to be precisely equivalent to the EPA's action at Valley of the Drums: locking the gate to a nonexistent fence. It keeps out motor vehicles on roads. Everything else in the world simply goes around.

There is a simple, one-sentence statement that neatly summarizes all of these points. It is this: *if wilderness works, what is this mountaintop doing outside it?*

I am not unaware of the good that environmental protection has achieved; I worked in the movement, after all, for more than twenty-five years. By creating preserves we have stopped dams and roads and clearcuts and thus kept many natural areas intact which would otherwise have been fragmented and lost. But it is time to recognize that all we really have been engaged in, in this pursuit, is a holding action. We have bought some time. Now we must use it.

Before we can begin this use, though, we who care for the earth are going to have to conquer an enemy more implacable and destructive than any logger or miner or developer we will ever face. That enemy is our own history. Hershberger Mountain's shadow lies long over the forest at its feet; but there is a valley in the western Sierra which casts a shadow that is far, far longer. Most environmental activists will easily recognize its name: Hetch Hetchy. And since the history of Hetch Hetchy is intertwined closely with the history of Hershberger Mountain—and with the Rattlesnake Epiphany—it seems appropriate to repeat its story here.

In the early years of the twentieth century, the environmental movement split messily into two warring camps. On one side were the preservationists, who believed that large blocks of land should be set aside and left pretty much completely in the hands of natural forces; on the other side were the utilitarians, who argued that the best way to protect natural resources was to make sure they were always used in a carefully sustainable manner. Both sides were vehemently opposed to cut-and-run forestry, minerals exploitation, overgrazing, and all the other abuses that were—and are—heaped constantly on the American land in the name of "freedom" and "progress." Both also insisted that government intervention was necessary. The preservationists, however, thought intervention should come in the form of absolute bans, while the utilitarians argued that what was needed was regulated use. The preservationists found their chief spokesman in John Muir. The utilitarians found theirs in Gifford Pinchot.

On the surface, at least, the two men could hardly have been less alike. Pinchot was a patrician, the son of a wealthy merchant; he grew up in privileged surroundings in New York City and on his father's large country estate near Milford, Pennsylvania. Muir was a peon, the son of a dour, natical Scots farmer who brought his family to Wisconsin when John was eleven; the future naturalist's boyhood consisted mostly of unremitting farm work interlarded with substantial doses of the strap whenever he fell off his father's extremely demanding standards. Pinchot attended private schools, graduated from Yale University, and spent a year and a half in Europe studying forestry at the French Forest School in Nancy and under the private tutelage of Sir Dietrich Brandis, the former Inspector General of Forests for the British colonial government in India. Muir had almost no formal schooling, and for most of his youth was allowed no reading matter but the Bible. (In later years he loved to recount how he had finally convinced his father that, since the old man could not read Scripture without his spectacles, an optics textbook could hardly be considered the work of the Devil.) Pinchot was always immaculately groomed, with a pencil-thin mustache and a prediliction for expensively tailored clothing; he moved through the upper-crust social gatherings that both men found themselves thrust into with the ease that comes only from long breeding. Muir had the wild hair and tangled beard of a Biblical prophet, and he preferred the feel of homespun to silks and linens. Though he eventually married into modest wealth, and amassed a bit more for himself, his role in society was always that of the tolerated, eccentric outsider.

Deeper down, though, Pinchot and Muir showed striking similarities. Physically, they were built along nearly identical lines—tall, slender, and wiry, with enough stamina to out-hike almost everyone on the globe except each other. They shared a deep love for the outdoors and a nearly equal disdain for those who would carelessly damage it. And both were charismatic leaders with the ability to rally others easily to their cause. When they cooperated—as they usually did, at least in the beginning—they could generate a momentum that was nearly unstoppable. When they came into conflict, sparks flew, and the heat is still being felt today.

The breach came at Hetch Hetchy. Widely regarded as a "second Yosemite," the canyon with the odd, scratchy name lay in the west-central Sierra a few miles to the north of what has since come to be called the "Incomparable Valley"—close enough that it was included in Yosemite National Park when the park was formed in 1890. Sliced through the same dazzling, light-gray granite, trending the same slightly south-of-west direction, the two valleys shared a common geologic history of river downcutting through a fracture zone, followed by glaciation and, for a time, life as a lakebed. Each had thus developed a flat floor across which a small, clear river meandered through bright meadows, surrounded by immensely tall, nearly perpendicular walls of polished rock laced by numerous waterfalls. Of the two, Yosemite was clearly the finer; but it was equally clear that, had Yosemite not existed, Hetch Hetchy alone would have been reason enough for the park's creation.

But Yosemite did exist; and because of this, Hetch Hetchy was deemed expendable, a mere copy of a masterwork which could be tattered and despoiled because the original was still safe in the gallery. In 1901, barely eleven years after the formation of the park that had protected it "for all time," the Second Yosemite was claimed as a municipal water-supply reservoir by the city of San Francisco. The battle over that claim lasted twelve more years, with Muir and the fledgling Sierra Club on one side and Pinchot and his utilitarian allies on the other. Three times the city submitted its application and saw it beaten back by Congress and the courts. The fourth time it prevailed. On December 19, 1913, President Woodrow Wilson signed the Raker Act, allowing water development to take place inside the park. Construction started within months; ten years later the dam was completed and the valley was dead.

Muir died first. Broken by the Hetch Hetchy battle, he passed away quietly on Christmas Eve, 1914, in a Los Angeles hospital, with the dam still not much more than a scratch in the surface of his beloved Sierra. Pinchot lived on another thirty years, having—one suspects—a few second thoughts. His autobiography, *Breaking New Ground*, completed shortly before his death in 1946 and published posthumously in 1947, mentions Muir several times, always admiringly. It doesn't mention Hetch Hetchy at all.

The specter of Hetch Hetchy, looming large as it does at the end of Muir's life, has created an image of Pinchot and Muir as distant antagonists who avoided each other's company. In truth they were good friends who hugely enjoyed traveling together. Since Muir lived in the west and went east only when duty forced him to, while Pinchot lived in the east and came west only when duty allowed, there were far fewer of these travels than either man probably wished for. We know, in fact, of only two. One was in 1899, when Pinchot sought Muir's advice on the fate of the giant Sequoias and ended up coming to San Francisco and touring the Caleveras Big Tree Grove with Muir and C. Hart Merriam, the founder of the United States Botanical Survey. The other—and by far the longer—was three years earlier, and much of it took place right here.

Perhaps that last statement is a bit misleading. It was not *right* here; as far as we know, neither Pinchot nor Muir ever climbed Hershberger Mountain. They did, however, pass very near its eastern flank. Standing on this rock-garden of a ridge, I can make out most of their route. The basin of the upper Rogue, through which they traveled, fills the void at my feet, dark green and lovely though terribly scarred by the spoor of the type of industrial forestry of which both men so strongly disapproved. The rim of Crater Lake, where they camped, crowns the eastern horizon. Our weather is better than theirs. Our weather is, in fact, splendid. Theirs was rain. Which, judging from their separate accounts, doesn't seem to have bothered either of them in the slightest.

The 1896 trip was a field expedition of the National Forest Commission, a federal study panel set up in February of that year by the National Academy of Science after a long period of prodding by Pinchot and Dr. Charles S. Sargent. Sargent, the curator of Harvard's botanical museum and one of the country's most respected naturalists, was the commission's chair; Pinchot was its secretary. There were five other members, making a total of seven. Muir was to have been the eighth, but he had declined. He felt that he could better serve the body as guide and unofficial adviser.

Muir and the commission—all except Pinchot, who was already in the field—met in Chicago in early July and headed west. Pinchot met them in Belton, Montana, where he and Muir had only a short time together before the Unofficial Adviser had to leave the party and head home to California on family business. He rejoined the commission in late August, in Oregon, traveling up from San Francisco and intersecting their route at the railway station in Ashland— as it happens, just six blocks from the home Melody and I have occupied for the past twenty-five years. They left immediately for Crater Lake by way of the highway now called Dead Indian Memorial Road, over the Cascades to the Klamath Basin and thence north. Tourists cover that route today in a little over two hours. It took the commission three days.

The weather was gray and blustery and threatening. They descended the wall of the Rim. The idea was to take a boat to Wizard Island. They never got there: halfway over, rain started and whitecaps kicked up on the lake's normally serene surface, breaking over the bow and threatening to sink the distinguished federal study group to the bottom of the deepest body of water in North America. Back on shore the others huddled under a grove of trees while Muir and Pinchot climbed a short distance to a large, flat boulder and built a defiant fire. The rest of the party might have had their enthusiasm dampened, but neither Muir (who had once responded to an earthquake in Yosemite by shouting joyfully "Noble earthquake! Noble earthquake!" and running out into the middle of a meadow in order to better experience it) nor Pinchot (who, in the same Incomparable Valley a few years later, had walked unhesitatingly under the edge of Yosemite Falls in order to find out what a river feels like after it has dropped a quarter of a mile) were going to let a little rain get in their way.

After a couple of hours the rain stopped, but the waves were still high and the hour was late. The bedraggled commission abandoned their island excursion and straggled back to the Rim, where their tents had been pitched. "Heavy rain during the night," Muir noted laconically in his journal. "All slept in the tents except Pinchot."

The next day it drizzled; but the day after that was brighter. They came down the upper Rogue past Hershberger, engrossed in conversation that Pinchot later recalled as "worth crossing the continent to hear." Forty-five miles from the lake, near the current location of Lost Creek Dam, they stopped for the night with an old Scots farmer named Gordon. Most of the party availed themselves of the hospitality of the house. Muir and Pinchot found a hay mow, burrowed into it, and spent the night there. It was beginning to become a pattern.

Now it was Pinchot's turn to be absent. Following—one suspects—Muir's advice and directions, the eminent forester headed south to the Sierra, where he spent ten days backpacking through the high country alone. "It was," he wrote, "a journey beyond my power to describe—from bare rocks and snowdrifts and glacial lakes and wind-twisted Pines and Cedars at timber line down to magnificent huge Sequoias and Sugar and Ponderosa Pines and Firs and Incense Cedars, down again to Digger Pines and out into the chaparral, and so at last to the vines and orchards of the San Joaquin Valley around Visalia." Muir, meanwhile, was guiding the rest of the commission through the coast redwoods, the Bay Area, and some of the tamer portions of the Sierra. Pinchot met them in Los Angeles, and they immediately headed east to Arizona—and the Grand Canyon.

What followed was recalled later by both men as one of the most memorable days of their lives. While the rest of the party allowed themselves to be driven by carriage to some of the South Rim's "scenic points"—the disdainful quotation marks around that phrase are Pinchot's—the Preservationist and the Utilitarian hiked out together along the lip of the immense and otherworldly void. "Standing with our heads down brought out the colors," wrote Muir: "— reds, grays, ashy greens of varied limestones and sandstones, lavender, and tones nameless and numberless." "I remember," added Pinchot, "that at first we mistook for rocks the waves of rapids in the mud-laden Colorado, a mile below us. And when we came across a tarantula he wouldn't let me kill it. He said it had as much right there as we did."

A storm like the one at Crater Lake had come in, and gray clouds played over the gorge, alternately highlighting and veiling the impossible country beneath the Rim. The temperature dipped toward freezing. It was time to return, but neither man was ready. Though they had no camping equipment—nothing, in fact, but the clothes on their backs, the contents of their pockets, and the remnants of the small lunch the hotel kitchen had prepared for them—Pinchot proposed that they spend the night on the edge of the chasm. Muir had been thinking the same thing. They found a tight little grove of cedar and burrowed into it, pulling down boughs for bedding and building a fire for warmth. Shadows cast by the fire were swallowed up in the great black Shadow of the canyon. Stars came out. The small pockets of rain left from the storm froze to the rock. Muir and Pinchot talked—and talked, and talked. Finally, around midnight, as both would recall later, the talk, though not finished, faded quietly into sleep.

Around 4:00 a.m. they awoke. The fire had died, and the cold could no longer be kept at bay. Rising, they scuttled through the freezing predawn darkness toward the hotel. By 4:30 they were sneaking inside "like guilty schoolboys"—the phrase is again Pinchot's—where they sat down to breakfast with the members of the search and rescue party that was being assembled to go out and look for their bodies.

Five years later came Hetch Hetchy, and the schism.

It is easy enough to second-guess, today: easy to point to other sites for San Francisco's reservoir, easy to bemoan the loss of the Second Yosemite at a time when it is desperately needed to take some of the intense tourist pressure off the first one. It seems clear that Muir saw the future more plainly than did Pinchot. Now it is needed, Hetch Hetchy is gone. The preservationist approach would appear to be thoroughly vindicated.

Alas, it is not that simple. Truth is always complicated and messy, and whenever you think you have a handle on it the stuff heads off in several different directions at once. The trouble with events like the Hetch Hetchy battle is that they tend to polarize people around separate viewpoints which, once defined, harden into ideologies. Ideologies, of course, attract ideologues. And of all the ugly things in the universe, the ugliest is an ideologue with his or her hands on public policy.

Muir and Pinchot probably wished—in the afterglow common to all such events—that their Grand Canyon conversation could have gone on forever. And so should we all. For the fruit of such a conversation might have been a synthesis, a forging together of thoughts wrought separately but actively intertwined. Preservation and utility are opposite sides of the same coin, distinct but inseparable. If you do not preserve something, you cannot use it. If you do not use it, there is no point in preserving it.

The demon spawn of Hetch Hetchy is the very thorough obfuscation it has brought to this point. Utility is now lumped with destruction, as if to use something you had to despoil it. Preservation is linked with purity, as if to preserve something you had to hermetically seal it. To follow that model is to create a world split equally between toxic waste dumps and museums. And there is not a whole lot of life in either place.

❦

We stop for lunch in the flowers. Paintbrush; asters; columbine; biscuit-root. A few phlox, left over from an earlier season. Where the ground is damp, mimulus and the faded remnants of fawn lilies; in the tight little groves of twisted fir and hemlock, trillium—once white, now shocking pink with age—and both false and true solomon-seal. The ridge's rocky spine thrusts up through the flower-spangled greenery, dropping off steeply into the big views. Ahead, a knoll, girt by a grove almost big enough to be termed a forest; beyond, out of sight from our lunch spot, a small dip, then a final spire of sharp, hard andesite; the mountain's crown. Surely no reasonable approach to protection of the Rogue-Umpqua Divide would have left this splendid mountaintop unprotected! Therefore the Wilderness Act must be, *ipso facto*, unreasonable.

I want to talk about reason, and about its role—or the lack of its role—both in the modern environmental movement and in the array of forces that the development community has ranged against environmental protection. First, though, I want to talk about the Warner Mountains. I want to do this because there is something in the Warners which demonstrates, even more clearly than the political severing of this mountaintop from the rest of the Rogue-Umpqua, the garden path down which the wilderness concept has led us.

I would like, for the sake of a smooth transition here, to be able to state that you can see the Warners from the summit of Hershberger. Unfortunately you can do no such thing. The Warners lie nearly 150 miles southeast of our ridgetop lunch spot, in the extreme northeastern corner of California, and even if the High Cascades were not in the way, the curvature of the earth would be. Still, as we lay out the bread and cheese and the crisp, succulent apples we have brought up here by car and knapsack, I cannot help gazing in that direction. The Warners are one of those places that are worth seeing again and again, if only as an indistinct spot on a guessed-at, far horizon.

This story really starts, though, in Yreka, California, on a winter weekend many years ago. Yreka is a small mining town just south of the Oregon/California border on Interstate 5, almost as far from the Warners as is Hershberger Mountain, and on that weekend in 1972 it was the unlikely setting for a bi-state conference of environmental activists— some from as far afield as Sacramento and Portland—who had come together to discuss the common problems of the border region. I was one of the Oregon delegates, and I still remember clearly the stir that went through the group when one of the Sacramento people announced that he had recently seen fresh logging scars within the boundaries of the South Warner Wilderness.

The South Warner is remote and little-used anyway, and the man from Sacramento had chosen a trailhead that was even more remote and little-used than usual. He was barely a quarter mile in when he came across the clearcut. It lay at the head of a high, north-facing valley, above a little trickle of water that was the source of a stream called East Creek, and its stumps and culls were still oozing sap. The Wilderness Act was at that time eight years old, and South Warner was one of the "instant wildernesses" the Act had created; before that it had been an administratively designated Forest Service Wild Area. Both of those categories were supposed to preclude logging. What was this abomination doing here?

Given the activist mindset, it should not surprise you that what we decided, there in Yreka, was that the Forest Service was trying to put one over on us. Many of the agency's timber managers were known to be unsupportive of the wilderness concept and resentful of the actions of the Outside Agitators in Congress and the environmental movement who had locked them out of large portions of their own forests. Clearly, we thought, one of those surly fellows had chosen this overlooked portion of an overlooked wilderness to test whether logging within it would be overlooked as well. We would pick up the gauntlet. The man from Sacramento was requested to contact Modoc National Forest, within whose boundaries the South Warner lies, and launch a strong formal protest. A month or so later I heard that this had been done. Then I lost track.

Late in the spring of 1992, in the wake of the Rattlesnake Epiphany, I found myself thinking once more of the Warners. What had happened to that protest? I phoned Modoc National Forest headquarters in Alturas, California, and, in a nice bit of symmetry, found myself speaking with a young woman named Betsy Ballard whose father, Jack, had been an activist friend of mine in the early seventies. (I am almost certain, in fact, that he was one of those present at the Yreka gathering.) The intervening twenty years had seen a nearly complete turnover in the Modoc National Forest staff, and the documents from that period were long buried, but Betsy offered to poke around a bit and see what she could find. A few days later I received a bulky package from her in the mail. Shortly afterward I headed for the Warners.

The Warners are spectacular. Forty miles long but never more than a few miles wide, they thrust above the high lava plains of northeastern California like a miniature Sierra. Their highest summits reach to nearly ten thousand feet and bear the prominent tooth and claw marks of ice-age glaciers. I found a large lake called Clear (it was) tucked behind a landslide-created dam low in one of the west-facing valleys, beneath towering, forest-clad walls of mountain. I found an immense, south-facing glacial basin called Homestead Flat (it wasn't) ringed by barren peaks, edged by aspen, and floored by hundreds of slanting acres of streamlet-laced buttercups. I found several well-maintained campgrounds which were, this warm weekend in late May, almost completely empty. I found high crags crowned by mountain mahogany which looked up to even higher crags crowned by nothing but snow and rock.

And I found the East Creek clearcut. It lay at an elevation of nearly 8,000 feet on a southern shoulder of the range, tucked over a ridge where it was invisible from almost everywhere but the East Creek trail itself. The trail, however, went right through it. It had been logged in the summer of 1972, and it must have looked like bloody hell when the man from Sacramento stumbled across it a few weeks later. The twenty years since, however, had softened it considerably. The edges were ragged; the hillside bowl that held it was bright with grass and wildflowers; and were it not for the remains of the stumps and culls—now whitened and going slowly to earth—it could have been mistaken for a natural opening. Those who sought industrial-forestry ugliness would not find it here.

But there was another thing they wouldn't find here, as well. They wouldn't find reprod. "Reprod" is foresters' shorthand for reproduction, the seedlings and young trees whose presence guarantees that a harvested area will once again some day be a forest. There were very few of them on these cutover slopes above East Creek. The opening made by the clearcut was still very much an opening, and was likely to remain so for the forseeable future.

The wilderness invasion had turned out to be an honest error. The bulky package from Betsy contained the evidence, in the form of a thick report to the Forest Supervisor from a field team sent to investigate our complaint. What they had found was relatively straightforward. The boundary of the South Warner Wild Area—the administrative predecessor to the Wilderness—had been drawn at a spot called "The Breaks," a band of low cliffs where the gentle terrain at the upper end of East Creek suddenly drops over into the canyon. The Wilderness boundary lay nearly a half-mile further south; it had been created as a straight line-of-sight survey from knob to knob along the ridge separating East Creek from Patterson Meadow, and between the knobs it conformed to nothing but the surveyors' imaginations. The timber manager had carefully laid his sale just outside the wilderness boundary, but he had chosen the wrong boundary. He had assumed—logically but, as it turned out, wrongly—that when Congress converted the Wild Area into a Wilderness they wouldn't change its shape. Thus the problem had boiled down, not to too much guile, but to too much innocence.

So the boundary flap had died down. Not, however, without serious consequences. The argument over whether or not a preserve had been purposely invaded had raged loudly enough to obscure a much more significant question: *What was logging doing so high on the south slope of the Warners in the first place?* The forests of the Warners are relict stands, remnants of a much greater postglacial woodland that retreated to the mountains as the climate warmed and dried. Especially at this elevation, they are fragile things which, once cut, have a less-than-average chance of coming back. Forestry here is not farming, but mining. One doubts seriously that the utilitarian Pinchot, with his strong belief in sustained yield, would have approved.

Each time you create a preserve, you also create a corollary: an unpreserve. The line you draw on the map destroys as well as protects. What lies within the line is, by definition, that land which society values more; therefore, what lies outside the line must be, by the same definition, that land which society values less. And this implies that we can log the hell out of it. In fact, it not only implies this, but actively encourages it. It does this in two ways. By forcing logging into a smaller physical area, it requires loggers to cut more intensively and to enter more marginal environments in order to produce the same amount of timber. And by grabbing land from the timber base it creates a Maginot-line mentality among forest managers, a sense that if the enemy is not halted at the current border the entire forest will shortly be overrun. There is only one way to permanently halt the expansion of a preserve, and that is to log the area it would expand into. The person who jammed the East Creek sale right up next to the wilderness boundary may not have been consciously thinking, *Well, that ought to stop the bastards*, but something similar to that cannot have been too far beneath the surface of his mind.

Ignoring the ramifications of an action is supposed to be the hallmark of resource abusers, but we in the environmental community have proved all to good at it ourselves. Wilderness is one example; there are plenty of others. A thing we have done in the name of open-space preservation, for example, is to encourage large-lot zoning. The unavoidable result of this is suburban sprawl, as the same numbers of houses are forced to spread out over a much larger area. Despite the clear correlation between these two factors, however, it is still the developers, who are supposed to love sprawl, who push small lots, and the environmentalists, who are supposed to hate it, who push the big ones. We have encouraged harvesting the wind as a substitute for the messy nature of combustion plants and nuclear reactors; the fruit of our labor has been wind farms sprawled over hundreds of acres of hitherto wild lands in the American Southwest, cleaner than the coal burners and nukes they replace, but considerably more ugly and invasive. In 1973, when the OPEC oil embargo hit, ways to use that event as a means of demonstrating the reality of resource depletion to an unbelieving public were a constant agenda item at environmentalists' gatherings; and I can still remember clearly the sense of disjuncture I felt as, traveling from Ashland to Portland for meeting after meeting, I was making a seemingly endless series of 600-mile round-trip drives to talk about ways to convince people to use less gasoline.

The consequences of an action will not fail to take place merely because we have not anticipated them. Therefore we must learn to anticipate as many as possible, so that we will not be surprised and displeased when they appear.

In the summer of 1978, in Niagara Falls, New York, the mess at Love Canal was uncovered and the entire environmental community went ballistic—with good reason. The buried canal held more than 280,000 tons of the deadliest kinds of chemical wastes known to humankind; it lay beneath a child-filled suburb and an elementary school, and it was beginning to leak. Toxic pools of green liquid were bubbling up in basements; the cancer rate had shot up to 250 times the national average, and miscarriages and birth defects had become commonplace. Drainage from the affected area entered the Niagara River a short distance above the famous waterfall. A Canadian study showed that cancer rates were dramatically elevated in the city of Niagara Falls, Ontario; the carcinogen was subsequently identified, firmly and unequivocally, as the mist from the falls. Significant concentrations of hazardous chemicals were beginning to be measured in the oceanic expanse of Lake Ontario itself. There was no wolf being cried here; the damage was very real, very frightening, and very big. Action was clearly required.

In the summer of 1987 I toured the Love Canal site with a party from the environmental group Great Lakes United, whose annual convention was being held that year at Niagara Falls. We were taken by bus to the dump site, where we viewed the stacked-up barrels and the boarded-up houses and the cyclone fence around the big, grassy space that used to be a school. Then we were driven north, down the Niagara Escarpment and out toward Lake Ontario. In twenty minutes or so we pulled up at another big, grassy space surrounded by cyclone fence. This was the Model City waste-disposal facility, and this, it turned out, was where the junk dug out of Love Canal had been shipped. Model City was state-of-the-art, with multiple impervious linings, and ponds full of faculative bacteria for modifying some of the more hazardous materials into less hazardous ones, and activated-charcoal filters, and ion-exchange filters, and everything else the creative human mind could come up with to take care of its garbage. But it was still a dump, and it was still in the Lake Ontario watershed. There is a truism in the toxic-waste business: *all dumps eventually leak*. The wastes would no longer be flowing over Niagara Falls. That was a definite plus. But the only difference, as far as Lake Ontario itself was concerned, was a matter of time.

I believe it is fair to ask, under the circumstances, just what it is we think we have gained. Digging something we don't want out of the ground, trucking it around long enough to create a potential for hazardous-materials release via traffic accidents, and burying it in the ground again in the same general vicinity that we dug it up from, simply does not strike me as a particularly rational approach to environmental management. It is not really doing anything to solve the problem. All it is doing is playing a massive game of musical chairs.

The environmental community has a full set of gods and ghosts and demons, and though we are quite good at going after the evil spirits of developers and industrialists we rarely exorcise our own. There is this thing about any well-developed mythology: those who hold most tightly to the myths are least likely to recognize them as such. And in a world increasingly in need of solutions rather than rhetoric, this lack of recognition becomes more and more dangerous. If we are going to survive on this planet, we are going to have to understand how the planet actually operates. Guesswork and good intentions will no longer do the job.

I am unsure precisely where to start the next part of the discussion. Perhaps, since we are eating lunch, the best place to begin is with diet. I hold in my hand a bit of bread and cheese; in the knapsack, waiting to be consumed at the end of the meal, is an apple. Is there anything wrong, environmentally, with this picture?

There are those who would argue that there is. Cheese is an animal product. A significant—and, I am afraid, growing—segment of the environmental community insists that the only diet compatible with proper care of the planet is strict vegetarianism.

The problem with this is that it ignores biology. We humans are omnivores; we have an omnivore's dentition, an omnivore's enzyme system, and an omnivore's gut. The range of essential amino acids we require for standard cell maintenance and replacement is structured around the consumption of at least small amounts of animal protein. It is true that it is possible, by careful monitoring, to obtain all your essential amino acids from plants; but the fact that it requires careful monitoring should tip you off to the fact that it is unnatural. If the thing is to protect nature, keeping ourselves on an unnatural diet seems at best an odd place to start.

It is unquestionably true that Americans eat more meat than is good for them, and that using animals for food can cause serious environmental harm. I am not arguing these points. I am simply saying that eating *no* meat is equally bad for us, and that using *no* animals for food can also cause serious environmental harm. Animal population dynamics are geared to what ecologists refer to as *environmental resistance*, a blanket term that encompasses all those forces in an animal's environment—climate, food availability, competition, and so forth—that tend to keep its numbers from expanding. Predator pressure is a major part of environmental resistance. If humans stop being predators, predator pressure will go down, environmental resistance will drop with it, and animal populations will respond by going up. Anyone who thinks this can be done without serious risk to the environment that the populations inhabit needs to do a little more reading in ecology.

Actually, a good case can be made that the apple in my knapsack poses more of a threat to Hershberger Mountain than the cheese I am eating, or the hamburger I intend to purchase on the way home. That is because this particular apple is not a native North American species; and lurking there in that nylon bag, waiting to be bitten into, it is still very much alive and capable of reproduction. Should I leave it here in a properly sheltered spot, there is a good chance it will grow. If you want to see one possible outcome of that harmless-sounding little scenario, go down to Georgia or Alabama and take a good long look at the kudzu.

Since the subject has come up, though, I should probably point out that there is a persistent myth surrounding the introduction of exotic species, too. The myth is that such introductions are always bad. The truth, as usual, is a little more complicated.

There is no question that bringing non-native species into a new environment is *often* bad. Kudzu, which began as an agricultural miracle crop before it turned into The Vine That Ate The South, is a prime example of this. So are starlings, and English sparrows, and the woolly adelgid and the gypsy moth, and star thistle, and Dutch elm disease. Certainly it is necessary to be aware of the hazards that foreign species with good adaptability and high reproductive potential can pose to the local flora and fauna. I think I have seen as much woolly mullein—a singularly ugly plant—as I care to be exposed to in one lifetime.

But that is only half the story. What about corn, a grass from the central Mexican highlands, grown all over the western hemisphere by the time Europeans arrived and since exported to the eastern hemisphere as well? What about potatoes, which grow naturally only in South America; or wheat and oats, which were originally found only in Mesopotamia? Virtually all crop plants are now grown in areas far removed from their ancestral stock; few have become problems (kudzu, a perfectly well-behaved field legume in Japan, is a notable exception), and there is little or no reason to ban their further importation.

Ornamentals show much the same pattern as do crop plants. A wide variety of trees and shrubs and flowers have been yanked up and carried halfway around the world by immigrants anxious to bring a little bit of the look of home into their strange new surroundings. A few of these have run amok—Scotch broom is a notorious example here in the Pacific Northwest—but the vast majority have stayed well-behaved. The English barberry in our yard poses little or no threat to its native relative, the Oregon grape; the Japanese maples planted in our city parks are not likely to displace the vine maples and bigleaf maples up here in the mountains. The Klamath plum (native) and garden plum

(European) that some previous resident planted next to each other beside our house are still coexisting quite nicely, thank you, and probably always will.

The blunt fact is that every species is an invader in the beginning. All lands emerge empty and build slowly toward paradise. The construction of an ecosystem does not take place through spontaneous generation—an exceedingly rare event in the planet's overall history—but through colonization and adjustment. Usually the adjustment process is gradual, but even in the absence of human help it can be strikingly abrupt. Many examples of these naturally supercharged ecosystems exist. The clearest is probably Isle Royale National Park.

If you were looking for the most thoroughly protected wilderness in the Lower 48, Isle Royale would certainly have to be high on the list. A rugged, forty-mile-long spine of greenstone and basalt thrust from the blue reaches of northern Lake Superior, it is separated from the nearest piece of the mainland—the Canadian shore of the lake—by fifteen miles of open water. What little settlement it had died out completely by 1892; in 1940 it became a National Park, to be kept forever wild, primitive, and undeveloped. The surrounding lake keeps it cold, and as a consequence the flora and fauna are boreal, more like those of Alaska than those of Michigan, of which it is nominally a part—a bit of the Far North plucked up and set down again, whole, on the rim of the North American breadbasket.

One of the great advantages of being an environmental writer is that you not only get to go to all those wild, exotic places you dreamed about seeing as a kid, you get to call this "work" as you do it. Thus it was that, in the summer of 1983, I spent three marvelous tax-deductible days canoeing Isle Royale in the company of an organic chemist and master canoe guide named Rod Badger. Putting in at Rock Harbor, a tiny outpost near the east end of the island, we paddled the length of Moskey Basin, a fjord-like arm of the big lake that runs behind islets and the peninsula for nine bright conifer-lined miles along the south shore. At the far end we set up camp on a small bit of soft earth between polished plates of elemental rock and spent the night listening to rain and loons. The next day we made two moderate-length hikes. The first took us from our Moskey Basin camp to Lake Richie, one of Isle Royale's multitude of cold, forest-girt interior lakes; the second led from Three Mile Camp to the summit of Mt. Franklin, 400 feet above Lake Superior on the island's rocky backbone. Both hikes took us through prime moose habitat; but, though we saw several sets of tracks and once came upon a pile of droppings ("moose berries," said Rod) fresh enough that they still steamed in the damp air, we caught no glimpse of the island's most famous inhabitants. The tourist from Detroit we met as we pulled the canoe out back at Rock Harbor on the third afternoon had been luckier. "I just walked a ways down the shore," he exclaimed, grinning broadly, "and there it was! Right on the trail! Biggest animal I ever saw!" The tourist was pale and soft-muscled from a desk job, and this little encounter with the ancient wild would probably keep him in conversational stock for many years.

Only it wasn't really the ancient wild. Wild, yes, but hardly ancient. Though they are natural inhabitants of the island—having made it there completely on their own, swimming across the broad strait that separates Isle Royale from Canada—their presence there dates back less than 100 years. When the copper miners that had tried, fruitlessly, to wrest a living from the island's tenacious deposits packed up and left for the last time in 1892, the large herbivore that characterized the place was the caribou. There was a small pack of coyotes which made part of its living from the caribou. The understory of the forest was thick with yew; the marshes and beaver ponds were broad expanses of pond lilies. An untouched natural wilderness, but far different from the one we know today.

It was the moose that made the difference. Striking out from the shore, probably as a result of population pressure on the mainland, the first moose made landfall on the island shortly after 1900. With no predators, their population quickly soared. (Coyotes, which can just barely handle a caribou, are no match at all for a moose.) By the 1920s the place had been pretty well eaten up, and the out-competed caribou were gone. So were the pond lilies and the yew. The moose began to starve. Several times over the next several decades moose populations crashed, only to rebound again as soon as the weary island flora started to recover.

Then, in the winter of 1949, another large animal made it to Isle Royale—this one across the ice when, during a particularly deep cold snap, the fifteen-mile-wide channel between the island and Canada froze over solid. The new arrival, the wolf, quickly killed off the resident coyotes and made itself at home. Wolves are considerably larger than coyotes, and they can handle moose quite nicely. The ecosystem was once again complete and in balance. It was a delicate balance—wolf and moose populations have both continued to fluctuate, sometimes wildly, to this day—but it was enough to allow the island flora to stabilize. Today you will see thimbleberry in the place of yew, and you will not see much pond lily. You will see no caribou and no coyotes. If you are lucky, like the man from Detroit, you may see a moose, or hear a wolf howl in the distance, as Rod and I did on one of our Moskey Basin nights. You will think you are in a place changed only by natural forces, and you will be right. But it is nevertheless a very different place than the one you would have seen as recently as a century ago.

The point that must be grasped is this: all things change. You cannot halt them by drawing boundaries around them and calling them wilderness. Even if you keep all things human out, you cannot do this. Nature will change on its own. You can welcome this change, or you can abhor it, but you cannot deny it.

You can, of course, attempt to deny it. But the attempt will be counterproductive. Because if you happen to be successful, what you will have accomplished is to replace natural fluidity with human-caused stability. You will, in other words, have inserted the human factor that you claim it is your intention to lock out. Absence of change is as great an aberration from the natural condition as anything the developers that we fight so proudly against could ever produce.

I have come to wish fervently that those well-meaning activists who prattle on about "ancient forests" would hie themselves to the nearest college and take a few courses in forestry. Forests are not ancient, they are new, every one of them, at every instant. Always being born; always dying; always *changing*. Ancient is for ruins and artifacts. What we have here is life.

We have come to the top of Hershberger.

The view is north. A void; a ridge; another void; and finally, flattened and far off, the insignificant hump of Rattlesnake Mountain. Through the binoculars I can just make out the trail switchbacking up its southeast face. There are flowers. I cannot see them from here, but I know they are there. We waded through them that day on the trail, knee deep, the grass still green though it was well into September. The summit was an island of grass and rock and little trees. Birds swam in the sea of air beneath us. Time stopped. I felt it stop, though I knew better. Perhaps it was the relative motion. You can fight time, or you can flow with it. Fighting it, you feel it pass. Flowing with it, you glide at its speed. It no longer passes, but accompanies.

I know the day ended, because eventually I found myself back in town. I went immediately—as always, after a hike—to a map. On the trail I rarely carry a guide; once I am home, though, I always want to know precisely where it is that I have been.

But this time the map seemed odd. The mountain was there—I could find that easily enough. So was the trail that we had climbed. What seemed to be missing was the trailhead—the trailhead, and the road to it. The road that fed that road wasn't there, either. There was, in fact, a vast swath of mountain space—a space I knew today to be crisscrossed with roads and marked by the mange of clearcuts that accompanies the fleas of industrial forestry—a space that was, when this map was drawn, as pure a *tabula rasa* as ever existed.

The map was dated 1965. I found another. This one was dated 1970, and all the roads were there. Five years was all it had taken. They had killed the wilderness in five short years. Who the hell did they think they were?

And then the epiphany flashed, and I knew the answer.

Who killed Cock Robin?
Who killed Cock Robin?
I, said the sparrow
With my little bow and arrow
It was I, Oh it was I.

We had been so damned smart. So smart, and so effective. We had passed the Wilderness Act and protected our little Edens and locked the bastards out. And the bastards, being human, had responded in kind. They had locked us out of what was left.

We had not only provoked this response, we had provided the tools for it. There is a clause in the Wilderness Act that states specifically that all roadless blocks of federal land that are 5,000 acres or more in size will eventually be considered for wilderness status. That was put there to expand the wilderness system, but it could also be used to block it. All the timber beasts had to do was go out there with their bulldozers and their chain saws and make sure there were no blocks of roadless land 5,000 acres or more in size left to protect.

Go to the archives in any National Forest you care to. Get out the maps. Watch the roads and harvest units advance. Up until about 1950 the movement will be practically nonexistent; this corresponds to the period in National Forest history when the timber companies were still cutting their own lands and were worried about competition from cheap federal trees. (It may seem inconceivable today, but there really was a time, not so long ago, when big timber companies actually campaigned actively *against* logging the National Forests.) From 1950 to 1965 the movement will proceed slowly but steadily, nibbling into the big blank areas on the map from their outside edges. Federal timber had begun to supplant private timber by this time, but its development was proceeding rationally, utilizing existing roads, going after easy-to-get trees. Keeping costs as low as possible. Doing exactly what you would expect from the laws of supply and demand.

In 1965, the picture suddenly changes. Roads explode, twisting out across the landscape like spaghetti; harvest units, and especially clearcuts, begin showing up in odd, distant places, widely separated from each other. By 1970, nearly all of the current National Forest road system is in place. Unprotected roadless areas large enough to qualify for preservation under the Wilderness Act have been reduced to a few mostly odd-shaped units lying primarily along ridgetops where there aren't any trees anyway. We disparaged those at the time as "rock and ice octopuses," but we were their underlying cause. Had logging remained economically driven, it would have continued to proceed logically in from the edges on a least-cost, most-profit basis. We had made logging political instead, and as a political tool it had been wielded very differently. We were displeased, which we should have been; and surprised, which we should not have been. We had used laws to make sure as much of the forest as possible would remain available for the purposes we thought forests should be used for. The timber beasts had used chainsaws and bulldozers to do precisely the same thing.

From the top of Hershberger we can see the top of Rattlesnake; the top, and part way down the south side, to about Windy Gap. We cannot see its base in the Fish Creek valley, we cannot see the Fish Creek road, and we cannot, thank God, see the clearcut. The one at the end of the road, near the head of the Fish Creek valley. The one they put the road in for, back in the late sixties; the one that followed immediately upon passage of the Wilderness Act. It is miles from any other logging activity, it took out marginal timber, like the East Creek clearcut in the Warners, and the only rationally defensible reason for its existence is to keep Fish Creek from becoming wilderness. In this it did not fully succeed. Political logging, like any other political activity, is subject to political responses. Logging invaded wilderness in the Warners; Wilderness would invade logging in the Western Cascades. When the boundary was drawn for the

Rogue-Umpqua Divide Wilderness, in 1984, it came up the valley on one side of the Fish Creek road, ran around the edge of the clearcut, and went down the valley on the other side of the road. The result is a long, skinny finger of unpreserved land with a big knob on its end thrust into the heart of an otherwise preserved valley, mad as a hatter but, from the standpoint of wilderness politics, perfectly rational. The Wilderness Act says that roads and clearcuts must be excluded from designated wilderness. It does not say what shape that exclusion has to be.

Oh, how I love wilderness, wildlands, roadless regions! How I love the timberline meadows, the tarns and rocks, the big views out over a land green as God intended! Further down are the forests, the trails winding among huge trunks, the sunlight hushed and filtered, a white river singing over rocks or curling, clear as a rain-washed sky, into deep pools beneath dark overhangs of moss-covered stone. If we are to keep life alive on this planet, our own lives included, we must protect such places, because it is there that life lives.

But we cannot protect life by preserving it. "Preserve" means to keep unchanged, and that is not protection, that is taxidermy. For that we could keep photographs. What we need is not just something to look at and enjoy knowing that it's there; what we need is something to be a part of. Not a specimen, but a dwelling-place. Not just to observe, but to live.

How do we make this happen? I confess I don't know. I know the path we have been on since Hetch Hetchy is not the right one, and I think I know roughly what the right one looks like, but I do not know how to get from here to there. As with forest fire suppression, which also began around the turn of the century, we have grabbed a tiger by the tail and must now find a way to let go without being eaten. Fire suppression has created a backlog of downed fuel, primed, dried and ready to flash into flame, so that when the spark finally comes (and the spark always finally comes) we get a great big fire that does all the work of the little fires that should have occurred over the last century, but with a lot more collateral damage. Wilderness preservation has created a backlog of downed greed. Because of this greed we cannot simply back away from the Wilderness Act. The collateral damage would get us. Nothing would survive the conflagration that would result.

So it is necessary, for the present, to maintain the wilderness system. It is even probably necessary to expand it in a few selected places. We cannot abandon the old safeguards until the new ones are up and operating. The Wilderness Act may have destroyed more wilderness than it saved—the patterns of logging since 1964 suggest precisely this—but to abandon it now would simply destroy the rest. We cannot do that and survive, at least not as anything remotely resembling the human race.

But this does not free us from the obligation to create new forms of safeguards. If anything, it makes the task more urgent. We are being forced to rely, more and more, on a tool that is demonstrably wrong for the job. The greater our reliance, the more glaring its weaknesses become, and the closer comes the time when it will no longer function at all. Now—while the dam is still holding back the tide—is the time to learn how to do without dams. After the floodgates have failed it will be too late.

Therefore, I would like to outline some principles, and suggest some possible directions in which they may lead.

The first principle is *inclusion*. Whatever solution we choose must include as many people, and as many points of view, as possible. The days of lockouts are over. There are too many of us on the planet, and too much demand for its limited resources—both tangible (wood, water, minerals) and intangible (solitude, scenic beauty, wholeness)—to continue to carve out separate bits for resource extraction and wildlands protection. No set of boundaries we could possibly draw would leave enough room on either side. The pressures for both of these things have grown high enough that, as long as each side excludes the other, both are going to continue to want it all; therefore exclusion can no longer be practiced. We must make ways to meet the needs of all of us from the same land base. Whenever I think about this, I find myself flashing to the moment in the 1992 Los Angeles riots when Rodney King, the rioters' nominal cause, went on TV to plead: *Can't we all just get along?* Perhaps we cannot. Certainly the time has come to try.

The second principle is *integration*. This follows logically from the principle of inclusion, but it stands on its own as well. It is not just a matter of integrating our separate human needs, but of integrating ourselves and our works—all of them—into natural systems. The "oneness with nature" that we in the environmental community continually say we seek cannot be achieved by walling off preserves and paving over the rest of the planet. That is separation, not oneness. Preserves are cages. It is time to tear down the bars and let the beast run free.

The third principle is *flexibility*. We must stop preaching purity and make sure, instead, that whatever we do leaves plenty of room to adapt. That is life's big secret, the principal reason that it has succeeded as well as it has. Adaptability breeds innovation; purity stifles it. And we need innovation. Every moment is different from every other moment; every square inch of ground is different from every other square inch. Our actions must alter to fit the moment and the milieu. Here on Hershberger I want to call your attention to the hemlocks. They are stunted, skinny, twisted; a caricature of the same tree further down the mountain. But their willingness to take this form is what has allowed them to survive. What would be the result if each seed demanded that its offspring grow straight and tall, like the hemlocks down by the road?

I do not mean to imply by this that the desired result is a form of nature that is stunted, skinny, and twisted. I do mean that we should allow natural values to flow into a shape that can survive, and that what survives in one place may very well not make it in another. Those who manage the land must be allowed the discretion to make the necessary choices. When Gifford Pinchot wrote the first "Use Book" for the fledgling Forest Service, he designed it to fit in the back pocket of a ranger in the field. Today its descendant, the *Forest Service Manual*, takes up an entire bookcase. There is no indication that this has improved the overall health of the National Forests. Faced with poor judgment on the part of our fellow humans, we have busily substituted rules. Better instead to increase the quality of judgment.

Inclusion; integration; flexibility. A good set of principles. How do we put them to work? How do we bring these admittedly overgeneralized ideas to bear on the highly specific problems that plague us without compromising the long-held goals of the environmental movement? Perhaps we should begin by reminding ourselves precisely what those goals are.

Though the language we have used to describe them has varied considerably from individual to individual and from age to age, environmentalists have always held a remarkably consistent set of goals. Muir spoke of "making all the land or garden instinct with God," and of the debt we owed to our "horizontal brothers." Modern activists are more likely to use phrases like "ecosystem integrity" and "endangered species," but the meaning is the same. We wish to protect wildlands; to clean up pollution, and prevent further pollution from happening; and to promote the use of resources in a sustainable, non-injurious manner, so that our children's children's children may enjoy the same level of abundance that we do. Every other goal we say we seek can ultimately be traced back to a footnote on one of these three.

I want to point to a central fact about these goals: *they are all human-centered.* I don't wish to belittle them by saying this, only to recognize the truth. Wilderness could not exist until civilization existed to compare it to. It is therefore a human-made phenomenon, and although protecting it will certainly benefit the other creatures who depend on it as well, our primary concern is with our own vested interest in the place. Pollution tends to be defined in terms of the harm it does to ecosystems, but what grabs our attention about it is that it is ugly and smelly, and our concern about ecosystem harm waxes and wanes suspiciously according to how much we happen to know about our dependence, as a species, on the particular ecosystem involved.

When Lake Erie nearly went belly-up back in the late sixties due to excess cladophora growth caused by phosphate pollution, what galvanized us into action was the imminent loss of fisheries and scenery and our own water supply. You would probably think it facetious of me to point out that the cladophora was doing very well indeed; yet cladophora is also a living thing, and from its standpoint the ecosystem was improving, not degrading. Should we therefore have let phosphate pollution continue? Obviously the answer is "no," but by saying this we abandon the cladophora, and thus explicitly void any claim we might have made to be protecting all of life. All means *all*, and that includes the cladophora—and the kudzu, and the woolly adelgid, and Dutch elm disease. These, too, are a part of life. There is clearly a difference between wiping out Dutch elm disease and wiping out, say, the spotted owl. One will lead the future of evolution in quite a different direction than the other. But from evolution's standpoint the two paths are equal in value. It is only from our own standpoint—ours, and the Dutch elm disease's and the spotted owl's—that there is any reason to care about which path we take.

And when we speak of sustainability we are clearly envisioning, first and foremost, the sustaining of our own species. If not that, what? Life itself is safe enough; we can change it radically, but we cannot eradicate it. It has been through many previous changes in the course of four billion years of earthly evolution, and will doubtless cycle through many more in the estimated twelve billion years remaining before the sun goes nova and the planet vaporizes. The disappearance of humanity and whatever large portions of the web we manage to take with us when we go will be no more than a blip on this curve. It obviously matters a great deal to us whether we live or die, and how well we live, and whether or not our species makes it through the next millennium. It is of very little consequence to whatever it is that will have taken our place in another sixty million years.

I am convinced that failure to acknowledge that what we call "environmental protection" is at heart human protection, and is the underlying cause for most of the trouble that the environmental movement finds itself in these days. We have set up a myth of envirocentrism, and we have fed it with other myths: the balance of nature, the evils of the marketplace, the noble savage living in harmony with the earth. In truth, nature is continually off balance—that's what keeps evolution moving forward and life living—and the forces which drive the marketplace, the laws of supply and demand, are merely human manifestations of the same biofeedback mechanisms which are supposed always to lead, among the "lower" life forms, toward ecosystem stability.

As for the Noble Savage, a glance at the fossil record should be enough to divest us of this nonsense. While it is true that many so-called "primitive" peoples have achieved a sort of rough truce with the earth, and that we can learn much from them, how they got there was through trial and error, and the errors were sometimes pretty big. It has long been recognized that ice-age hunters, here and in Europe, were a primary cause behind the disappearance of the mammoth and the mastodon. Paleontological evidence now also suggests overwhelmingly that the Polynesians—Gaugin's idyllic South Sea Islanders leading simple, harmonious lives with flowers in their hair—were directly responsible for the extinction of more than 2,000 bird species, an ecological slaughter unmatched by Europeans before the invention of firearms and the holding company.

Myth-creation is always a sign that we are too far removed from something we care very deeply about, and these myths, together with the myths of the other side—resource abundance, free enterprise, private property rights—are an indication (as if we needed another indication!) that we have severed ourselves too far from nature. In this the Deep Ecologists and their allies in the preservationist wing of the environmental movement are absolutely correct. They are also correct when they state that our best way out lies in emulating the ways of the North American Indians. This does not lead, however, where most of them seem to think it is going to lead.

Leaving nature at the mercy of natural forces was not the Native American way. The earth was sacred to their culture, but the wholeness of nature was not. Precolumbian America was not an untouched Eden, but a working landscape. Fire, often human-caused, kept the brush cleared and the grasslands open. Game was culled like farm stock, with an eye to the next generation, rather than merely being slaughtered under the assumption that there was always more over the next hill and anyway, the Lord would provide. Native Americans made extensive use of copper before Europeans did, but they stopped. This is generally attributed to a technological inability to work dwindling deposits, but this is a European-supremacy reason, and anyway, it is demonstrably false: the veins the Old Copper Indians mined did not stop where they did. I have picked metal out of them myself. I suspect the use of copper stopped—or died back; it never really stopped completely—not because they couldn't mine it anymore but because mining didn't fit in with their other management objectives. Mining messes up landscapes that might be better used for something else. When you are managing something as a whole rather than as bits and pieces you have to think that way.

That is the model we must emulate: an earth kept whole, not cut up by artificial boundaries; the stewardship of the good manager, not the hands-off harmony of the myth-maker. We must involve ourselves with nature, not stand back and admire it from afar. We need to get our hands dirty. The early preservationists were correct in assuming that what they saw was worth preserving. But what they saw was a working landscape. It has deteriorated on our watch, but we can get it back, not by bronzing it like baby shoes and placing it on the mantle, but by working it ourselves.

It is easy enough to see where resistance to this idea has come from. All you have to do is go to a clearcut, or a mine, or a raw subdivision sprawled across another thousand acres of forest or farmland. If you are at all tuned to wild values the sense you will get in such places is not only of loss but of sacrilege. The vandals have not just entered the cathedral, they have scattered the reliquaries and used the chalice for a chamber-pot. Standing amidst the carnage, shaking your fist, it is easy to find yourself screaming, *Never again*. Heave the heathen into the street. Lock the door behind them. Let only legitimate worshippers pass through.

But such a response—though perfectly understandable— is thoroughly off the mark. The environment is not a cathedral, but a community, and our place within it is defined, not by adulation, but by communion. We give to the community; we also take from it. We do not take more than our share, if we are ethical, but we do take. If there is damage it is because we have taken too much, or have taken it in the wrong manner, not because we have taken it at all. Nearly every environmentalist can misquote Aldo Leopold: *The land is not a commodity which we own, but a community to which we belong.* Few can quote the passage correctly:

> *Conservation is getting nowhere because it is incompatible with our Abrahamic concept of land. We abuse land because we regard it as a commodity belonging to us. When we see land as a community to which we belong, we may begin to use it with love and respect.*

Use it with love and respect. But use it. Abuse and use are not synonymous; you can, in fact, abuse something quite thoroughly without using it. It may be easier here to think, not of things, but of children. Child-protection laws recognize two distinct ways in which children may be abused. One is by actually hurting them, either physically or emotionally. The other is by locking them up.

"In wildness," wrote Henry David Thoreau, "is the preservation of the world." This is true, but it is only half the story. It is equally true that *in the world is the preservation of wildness.* The world and wildness are inextricably linked, yin and yang, spirit and substance, darkness and light. Each member of the pair helps to define the other. We cannot achieve the environmental balance we in the movement say we crave until all nature is seen to be simultaneously in the service of both. The utilitarian Pinchot called the road up Colorado's Pikes Peak "a scurvy thing to do to a great mountain." He was right. The preservation-minded Muir called for more roads in the high Sierra, in order to allow people better access to wild places. He was also right. Roads are utilitarian, but some roads have disutility; preserves are, well, preservationist, but too much preservation is an act of destruction. Always the excess must be avoided; always the balance must be sought. It is good to be angry at destruction. ("Moderation in all things," wrote James Hilton in *Lost Horizon*, "including moderation.") But we must not let our anger blind us to the fact that not everything humankind does to the earth—not even in the name of use—is destruction.

Hershberger Mountain here under my feet is sacred—as all land is sacred. It needs to be preserved—as all land needs to be preserved. The fact that I say *all* should forewarn you of what I am going to say next: preservation and use must henceforth take place at the same time, in the same places. This is impossible only so long as you consider preservation and use to be mutually exclusive concepts. See them as yin and yang. Then the picture will fit.

Therefore I propose the following:

Log all lands, but only in such a manner that no lands look or act logged.

Preserve all places, but only from damage, never from use.

It will take time to implement this scenario. Time, and constant guardianship. I suspect the job will never really be complete. There will always be some places where a heavier hand on the saw will seem appropriate; there will be other places, full of a sense of the sacred, where we shall continue to want logging and roads to stay out altogether. But these places should be small—rarely more than a few hundred acres—and widely scattered. Over the vast bulk of the land we should simply move lightly, taking what we need, leaving the web intact. Long harvest rotations should be the rule, and culling rather than clearcuts. Roads should be thought of, for the most part, as temporary structures, to be removed after use along with the machinery that uses them. Where reproduction cannot be reasonably guaranteed we should not log at all. But silviculturists—not politicians, not economists, not businessmen or activists—should be the ones who determine this.

I am painfully aware that what I have written here will cause many to accuse me of selling out. But you cannot sell what you have never owned, and none of us owns the land. Private and public property alike are an illusion. The land belongs only to itself. It will share its products with us—tangible and intangible, produce and wholeness, lumber and silence—but it will not be bound by our strictly human concepts of what it should do once the products are taken. In this it will always chart its own path. We can cooperate with it, or we can destroy it, but we cannot command it. Therefore choose cooperation.

Descending, in flowers. We move slowly southward down the hard backbone of the mountain, the big view before us. The lookout rides the southern prow of the ridge, a small white clapboard building on a green knoll, surrounded by space. No sign of Heidi and the goats, though they would hardly seem out of place here: otherwise, and at least for this instant, all is completely right with the world.

Some time ago I asked the rhetorical question: If wilderness works, what is this mountaintop doing outside it? The answer, of course, is that it isn't. The boundary excludes it, but boundaries are artifacts and therefore suspect. Nature ignores them. We are the only ones they fool.

> *. . . whether or not it is clear to you, no doubt the universe is unfolding as it should. Therefore be at peace with God, whatever you conceive Him to be.*

> — Max Ehrmann, *Desiderata* (1927)

The left hand of Eden packs a wicked punch, but it is no match for reality. Seek the real. Hold onto it. Mountains and flowers are real; more real, at least, than boundaries. Follow mountains and flowers.

Near the base of the ridge, almost back to the car, we pause briefly at a fork in the trail. The left branch leads to the top of the stairs; the right, to a new trail, cut to avoid stair-climbing, which makes a long switchback north and then south again along the meadow-hung mountainside. It looks far longer and more time-consuming than the stairs, and will take us to what appears to be quite far out of our path. Nevertheless, that is the way we choose to go.

Down the River

It is a cool morning in early March, and I am walking down the Rogue River trail in southwestern Oregon, in the wild canyon somewhere below the mouth of Grave Creek, knapsack on back and staff in hand, thinking about my yard. There is a light overcast, from which a few drops of rain occasionally fall. Rough walls of ancient greenstone press tightly against the river, rising to forested crests more than 4,000 feet above my head. The forest spills over the rim and down the walls, a feathering of dark green conifers on soil too steep to seem real. At some places the trees reach all the way to the water; at other places the rock is bare, or nearly so, for as much as a thousand feet up from the shore. The trail stays high, sixty feet or more above the river level in most stretches, alternately buried in trees and clinging to open, precarious ledges pasted to precipices over the whitewater. Every conceivable surface that is not beneath a tree holds either water or flowers.

My yard is nothing like this, of course, but it does have its moments. I am thinking particularly of the two plum trees outside the window over the kitchen sink. At this season they are in bloom, and when I sit at the table across the kitchen and look toward the sink, the window is filled with masses of small, bright blossoms. The trees are of two separate varieties. Each has white petals, but the centers of the flowers on the right-hand tree are deep red, while the centers of those on the left-hand tree are yellow. So the hue of the right-hand tree is pink and the hue of the left-hand tree is cream, though when the petals intermingle on the ground you cannot easily tell which is which.

Here in the canyon the predominant flowers are saxifrages, similar in color to the blossoms on my left-hand plum tree, but smaller and more delicate, with lacy, serrated petals. Standing in phalanxes along the ledges, marching single-file up the crevices, occasionally hanging upside down, they brighten every rock outcrop. On the banks of coarse soil between the outcrops they give way to scattered patches of lasthenias, the small sunflowers referred to locally as "goldfields" (or sometimes "Oregon sunshine"). The areas between the lasthenia patches look bare, but close examination proves that they are covered with the wiry stems and tiny white flowerlets of draba. A few clumps of shooting stars add accents of bright reddish purple, and in the disturbed ground beside the trail small, wild geraniums have occasionally taken root. These are purple as well. So are the rich clumps of Siskiyou penstemon—*Penstemon anquineus*, one of the few shade-loving members of that large genus— that carpet the moist green slopes beneath the trees.

The river is mostly white. It mutters and roars at the bottom of its deep cleft, complaining endlessly about the big rocks in its bed. This is one of the preeminent whitewater rivers of America, and in the summer you cannot walk very far along this stretch of trail without being passed by numerous rafts and drift boats and inflatable kayaks and even the occasional inner tube. Melody and I commonly see a few even when we are here in the winter. Today, unusually, there are none. There were only three cars parked ahead of ours in the lot that serves both the trailhead and the Grave Creek boat ramp, and all apparently belonged to hikers. This is a popular stretch of trail for day hikes: largely level, spectacularly scenic, and with a good turnaround point at Rainey Falls, just over a mile and a half in. Down the river and then back up. We have no particular plans to go that far; but then, we have no particular plans to stop before we get there, either. Chances are good that we will see the falls today.

The yard is beginning to flower. Along with the plums, there are daffodils on the front bank and tiny geraniums—*Geranium molle*, the same species we have been seeing here along the river—twined through the grass. The grass is greening up. The japonica, cut back and transplanted last fall and looking all winter like nothing much more than a bundle of dead sticks, has covered its naked branches with bright magenta blooms. Later will come the iris and the tulips and (if they have survived their own move) the day lilies. There will be tassels on the oak and the walnut, and the periwinkle vines will bear soft, blue blossoms an inch and a half across. The barberry is already in bud; soon its clusters of waxy yellow bells will brighten the fence along the south side of the back yard, beneath the hawthornes.

If I were not here on the Rogue, I would be working in the yard. There is much to do this season. The grass is not yet in need of mowing, but it will be soon, and the lawn must be made ready. The debris of twigs and small branches blown from the trees by winter storms must be picked up and disposed of; the building materials left over from various recent construction projects must be hauled off. Last year's oak leaves, left purposely on the ground all winter as a form of natural mulch, must now be raked. The periwinkle continues to invade the lawn; we beat it back throughout the spring and summer, but it never seems to lose as much ground as it has gained. One of these days we are going to have to rip it all out and start over.

I sometimes wonder why we humans bother with yards at all. Certainly they take much time and energy that could be used quite productively in other ways. Money, too: for seed and fertilizer, for garden tools, for water to keep the grass green and the flower beds moist and the decorative shrubs we have imported from wetter parts of the globe alive. Looked at objectively, yards simply do not make a great deal of sense.

And yet most of us have them. We keep our grass and our flowers and our trees, and we give up our weekends and run up our water bills, and we put setbacks in the planning codes to make sure our neighbors do the same. If there is no room for a yard—in a city apartment, say, or in a condominium—we still keep window boxes, or at least house plants. We establish large communal lawns in the form of city parks, and we pay people to make sure the parks are well kept. In a half-century of restless living, traveling by car through cities big and small in forty-six of the fifty states, I cannot remember ever seeing a parkless town.

I may be wrong, but I suspect that all of this has a great deal to do with the same impulse which has brought me to the river today. I think we humans have an innate need to stay in touch with life. We are a part of life, too, one small thread in the broad, green fabric of the biosphere, and if we have forgotten that with our minds we still remember it with our bodies and our souls. So we keep pets and plants, and we dig in the warm earth, and we picnic in the park on a summer Sunday, and we feel better for all of this: calmer, more relaxed, somehow more *whole*. The converse is also true, of course: take these things away from us, and you will make us feel *less* whole. We may or may not recognize the cause of our angst. The angst will be there anyway. Perhaps this is oversimplifying, but I strongly suspect that much of the alienation felt by our inner-city youth stems from the almost complete lack of green and growing things in their lives. If this is so, tending trees and grass in the ghetto could prove to be the most cost-effective crime-prevention investment we will ever make.

Opposite Sandersons Island the trail dips to river level, and there is a small beach among boulders. We pause for a bite to eat amid a flurry of light raindrops. Sharp, crumbly cheddar, coarse bread, and an apple and an orange are dug from the depths of the knapsack and spread out on a convenient flat rock. The river mutters past.

Sandersons Island is really just a very large gravel bar, several hundred yards across but only a few feet high and nearly barren of vegetation. The canyon walls rise precipitously around it. There is a small rapid at the head of the south channel, on the far side of the island; here on the north side the equivalent drop is at the channel's foot, just before the two branches of the river rejoin, so much of what we see from our improvised stone table is slack water. A small mixed flock of mergansers and Canada geese has touched down and the birds are mingling along the island's northeast edge, some on the water, others tucked into hollows in the pebbly shore. The mergansers are feeding like mallards, standing on their heads with their tails straight up, but through the binoculars I can see the white breasts of the males and the characteristic brown, shaggy heads of the females. The much larger geese look out of place. Eventually they separate from the mergansers, drifting downstream with the current and waddling back onto land just above the rapids, directly opposite us. There are three of them. Geese are grazers, among the few birds which have adopted that lifestyle, and while one beds down on the bank the other two wander inland toward the island's low crest, looking for grass. Even without the binoculars we can see the long white-banded necks curve down, the dark bills pulling at the few scraggly blades that the island supplies.

I wonder what would happen if we could bring ghetto kids out here, away from the concrete and the pavement and the stench of cars and people, into reality? Certainly it would improve their attitudes. I remember one visitor we brought to the river a few years ago. He was not a ghetto product headed for a life of crime—not, that is, unless you count poetry a crime—but he was a city boy, born and bred in Chicago and living then in New York, and we thought he could stand a good dose of green. We walked the south-side trail that day, down the other side of the river, through heavy, wet forest and along slick greenstone ledges. It was December, and it was raining, at times quite hard. We bundled into ponchos and ignored it. The canyon walls disappeared upward into swirling mists; every turn of the trail seemed to have its own waterfall, quickly soaking our boots and pantlegs. At Rainey Falls our visitor took off his hood and stood bareheaded in the rain at the brink of a rock, shouting lines of poetry I could not hear over the roar of the water though I stood barely ten feet away. We retraced our steps toward the car. The trailhead was nearly in sight again when he suddenly swung aside onto a flat point of stone thrusting out over a precipitous drop to the river. For a long while he stood there, slowly turning, taking in the wild, wet, cold, roaring, impossibly alive scene. Then he came back toward the trail, grinning broadly. "My girlfriend's been jealous of this trip, anyway," he said. "I'll have to tell her we had a terrible time. It rained all day. She wouldn't have enjoyed it at all."

That is all well, and I certainly would not want to deny city kids the opportunity to do these things; but the truth is, planting grass and trees in the ghetto would probably do more good. The greater need, these days, is not so much to set aside distant places as it is to improve access to nature where people already are. We need to be able to affirm our connection with the rest of life, not just yearly, or even monthly, but daily—hourly, if possible. We need to touch the web. This is a lesson that our culture has not yet learned very well. I cannot count the numbers of times I have driven for miles through stunning scenery with no place to pull off the road; have made for the one bit of greenery in sight only to be confronted with fences and "No Trespassing" placards; have stopped at "rest areas" where the forest is fenced out and the lawn is small to nonexistent and the only significant item in sight is the toilet. Our freeways have broad shoulders, but they are studded with signs that shout NO PARKING. Perhaps that should be taken as our national motto. Inscribe this statement around the Great Seal of the United States: BROAD SHOULDERS—NO PARKING.

It doesn't have to be this way. It does not. We have the means; we also have the will, if our national obsession with greenery in and around the house is any indication. What we seem primarily to be lacking is focus. In a typically American display of obsession with bigness, we have been looking over the top. The Wilderness Act is written specifically to ignore anything under 5,000 acres in size, and environmental groups tend to put their primary efforts into things much larger, even, than that. We worry about the Arctic Wildlife Refuge and ignore the vacant lot down the street, failing to understand that, of the two, the vacant lot may actually be the more important.

That may sound like I advocate breaking up large blocks of wildlands. I do not. These are important, too: otherwise, why would I have driven fifty miles to spend this damp day in one of them when there is work to be done in my own yard? There are no mergansers or geese in my yard, only scrub jays and starlings, and though the flowers may come close to these the scenery around them simply cannot compare. The level of integration I can reach between myself and the rest of the natural world is also deeper here. I will be much quieter in spirit tonight than I would have been had I merely worked in the yard. Sometimes, to paraphrase Canadian folksinger Stan Rogers, it is necessary to take big bites of the wild. Nibbling about the edges cannot always do the trick.

All this is true, but not particularly relevant. The fact is that if we cannot protect our access to the smaller areas, the larger ones probably will not have much of a chance, either. Rather than walk down the river we will be sold down it. If you live in a wooden house, you know you need lumber; if you drive a car you know you need petroleum. How can you know you need wild nature? Only through the same sort of daily contact. If you wish to protect the Arctic Wildlife Refuge, begin with your own back yard. Only after we reintegrate wildness into our cities can we hope to reintegrate our cities into wildness. We speak of nature as a seamless web; we should be handling it as such. As long as we treat it like a Christmas package, wrapping it up in ribbons and keeping it hidden in the closet until the holidays, both we and it are going to continue to be in trouble.

The rain is still light, but the rocks are beginning to become moist, and even the river looks damper. It may promise great things for the flowers, but it isn't doing much for the cheddar. We put the lunch away and scramble back to the trail, still headed downstream. Immediately around the next buttress the river goes slack and we become aware of a distant, chaotic rumble, like an imminent volcanic eruption or a deranged subway. In ten minutes we are at Rainey Falls.

The falls are not very high—perhaps twelve feet—but as a raw display of brute power they will certainly do until something better comes along. They carry the river's entire flow, and at this season especially that is quite an immense amount. The rough rim is horseshoe-shaped, like Niagara's; the river pours in a jagged white wall over all of it, meeting at the focus of the parabola in a deliriously loud tumble of noise and foam which takes hundreds of downstream yards to sort back out again into water and air. The rock beneath your feet trembles; you must shout to be heard, and even then there is no guarantee that your poetry will not be lost in the void.

We make our way over tumbled ledges of watersmooth rock to the edge of the slapping river, looking upstream into the maw of the falls. The rain has petered out, and the weak sun is trying to break through. A stick is caught in an eddy near my feet. I fish it out and heave it toward the swift center of the channel, where it bobs on the troughs and the swells, floating fleetly away. Down the river.

Back in my yard the plums and the japonica are in bloom and the grass leaps out of the ground and there is a mass and a chitter of starlings. The great web of life touches down there as well as here. Savor it all. Build it into your lives, city and suburb as well as wilderness. Integrate. The wild is wonderful, but the wild doesn't know it is wild: we are the only ones who know, or indeed who care. Let life live wherever it may find itself. Waste little time on creating preserves; it is not the wild that needs boundaries drawn about it, it is us. Let us draw those boundaries no larger than we must, and if the wet wild wishes to come within them, let us welcome it there as well. Protect nothing; venerate everything. Take what you need, but harm as little as possible in the taking. Stop the car and get out. Touch the grass, and the web closes; encourage small lives, and the large ones will be strengthened. We travel together down the river, and we can run such rapids as we must; our problems do not arise from whitewater, but from repeatedly trying to row upstream. Ship your oars and live.

Acknowledgements

I could not have created this book by myself. Fortunately, I didn't have to: valuable assistance was available from a number of sources.

The most important of these, as usual, was my wife, Melody. She always seemed to be around when I needed her to toss ideas back and forth, and her insights into the processes of nature as a trained biologist helped jump-start the work numerous times when its battery seemed to have died. Many of what pass for "my" thoughts here are actually hers, but they intertwine so thoroughly with mine I doubt either of us could separate them any more. I have written them in my own words. I make no such possessive claim for the ideas themselves.

Aside from Melody, the person who played the most active role in helping me shape the book was undoubtedly Tom Ward. Tom is a permaculture designer, a Quaker, and a lover of wild places whose ideas closely parallel mine, and talking them over with him through numerous lunches following Meeting for Worship was both clarifying and encouraging. I can't hope to pay him back, but I can dedicate this book to him, and I have done just that.

A number of others also contributed: it is possible to name only a few of them here. My colleagues on the Transition Team at the Rogue Institute for Ecology and

Economy were often supportive sounding boards: Howard LaMere, Cass Moseley and Melissa Borsting should be singled out especially in that regard. Alan Reder read the complete manuscript at an early stage and offered extremely helpful suggestions—it was he, for instance, who came up with the very apropos subtitle. (Melody and Tom also both read the complete manuscript, and some of their improvements in phrasing and structure are in there as well.) Ed Kupillas read the "Spotting the Owl" and caught me in at least one significant error (since corrected)—and Ed, I really enjoyed the coffee and the conversation afterward! We need to do that more often. Max Gartenberg's comments on "Hopeful Monsters" changed it from a helpless mishmash to a workable essay, and Max, if you didn't insist on living in New Jersey I'd suggest coffee more often with you, too.

Finally, I would like to thank acquisitions editor Warren Slesinger, managing editor Jo Alexander, and the entire Editorial Board at OSU Press, for offering constructive criticism and patiently working through the tantrums when I failed to take it constructively. There were plenty of times, following the cooling-down period after sending off yet another blistering piece of e-mail, that I was extremely glad they have worked with many other authors and are familiar with the shortcomings of the breed. I hope this book lives up to their well-demonstrated faith in it.

Notes on Sources

Epigraphs. The two epigraphs for this book come from William
   Butler Yeats, *The Celtic Twilight: and a selection of early poems*
   (New York: New American Library Signet Classics, 1962), p.
   34; and Henry David Thoreau, *Walden and Civil Disobedience:
   a Norton Critical Edition* (New York: W. W. & Company , ed.
   by Owen Thomas, 1966, hereinafter cited as *Walden*), p. 219.

p. xiv: The Pinchot quote is from Gifford Pinchot, *Breaking New
   Ground* (Washington, D.C.: Island Press Conservation Classics,
   1987, hereinafter cited as *Breaking New Ground*), p. 506.

p. 5. The Siddon quote can be found in more complete form in
   Art Wolfe and William Ashworth, *Bears: Their Life and
   Behavior* (New York: Crown, 1992), p. 198. The interview on
   which the quote was based was conducted on October 25,
   1990.

p. 11. (a) The quote beginning "The fortnight ending . . . ." is
   from Henry Beston, *The Outermost House* (New York: Penguin
   Nature Library edition, 1988, hereinafter cited as Beston), p.
   10.

   (b) The "night so luminous and still" and the quote
   beginning "There are nights in summer . . . ." are both found
   in Beston, p. 218.

   (c) The description of the Great Beach ("solitary and
   elemental . . . .") is from Beston, p. 2.

p. 14. The warning about Mt. St. Helens was printed in Cascade
   Section of the American Alpine Club, *Climber's Guide to the
   Cascade and Olympic Mountains of Washington* (Boston: The
   American Alpine Club, 1961), p. 5.

p. 15. (a) The Ballard quote comes from Robert D. Ballard, *Exploring Our Living Planet* (Washington, D.C.: National Geographic Society, 1983), p. 267.

(b) The "darkened, gouged-out stump" is found in Charles C. Plummer and David McGeary, *Physical Geology, 2nd ed.* (Dubuque, Iowa: Wm. C. Brown, 1982), p. 44.

p. 17. (a) James Hutton on the present and the past is quoted in Plummer and McGeary, *ibid.*, p. 17.

(b) Ellis Jump made his observations during Meeting for Worship at North Pacific Yearly Meeting's Annual Session, July 20, 1980.

p. 18. The familiar passage from the Book of Isaiah comes from Chapter 40, Verse 4.

p. 21. The long quote here is from Beston, pp. 220-21.

p. 32. "Ozymandias" is probably the most anthologized poem in English. I found it (this time) in Oscar Williams, ed., *Immortal Poems of the English Language* (New York: Washington Square Press, 1960), p. 295.

p. 39-40. I am indebted to Darwin Lambert's *Great Basin Drama: The Story of a National Park* (Niwot, Colorado: Roberts Rinehart, 1991) for the facts on which this blow-by-blow account of Prometheus's death is based.

p. 60. Wildlife "peaks" at you in the brochure "Welcome to the Lake Arrowhead Communities," Lake Arrowhead Communities Chamber of Commerce (undated, but probably 1991).

p. 68. (a) Francis Parkman, *The Oregon Trail: Sketches of Prairie and Rocky-Mountain Life*. In my edition (Boston: Little, Brown, 1922), the quote about "blighting the charm" is found on p. ix.

(b) The Oscar Wilde quote about killing and loving—from which the title of this essay is also derived—comes from "The Ballad of Reading Gaol," line 37: my source was Paul Robert Lieder, Robert Morss Lovett and Robert Kilburn Root, eds., *British Poetry and Prose, revised edition* (Boston: Houghton Mifflin, 1938), vol. 2, p. 890.

p. 70. (a) The chapter epigraph is from Edward Abbey, *One Life at a Time, Please* (New York: Henry Holt & Company, 1988, hereinafter cited as *One Life*), p. 127.

(b) The quote about the survey crew is found in Abbey's *Desert Solitaire: A Season in the Wilderness* (New York: Ballantine Books, 1971, hereinafter cited as *Desert*), p. 67.

p. 71. (a) Abbey's journal entry on sex and female nudity is quoted from *One Life*, p. 70.

(b) The "Pimpmobile" is in *Confessions of a Barbarian: selections from the journal of Edward Abbey*, edited by David Peterson (Boston: Little, Brown, 1994, hereinafter cited as *Confessions*), p. 342.

(c) Abbey's deprecatingly smug self-description ("cranky, cantankerous . . . .") is in *Confessions*, p. 308.

p. 72. (a) This description of Moab is from *Confessions*, p. 335.

(b) The bit about "Arches Natural Money-Mint" is found in *Desert*, p. 52.

p. 73. (a) The tourists are compared to turds in *Confessions*, p. 136.

(b) The "iron dinosaur" comes from *Desert*, p. 297.

p. 75. Abbey on *The Joy of Sex* is from *Confessions*, p. 241.

p. 77. (a) Abbey's advice about sharing joy with a child is from *One Life*, p. 63

(b) The joyful frogs are found in *Desert*, pp. 143-44.

p. 78. "Outdoors! Outdoors! . . ." comes from *Confessions*, p. 254.

p. 79. Abbey's ruminations on progress may be found in *One Life*, p. 60.

p. 80. This version of the Prayer of St. Francis is used as the epigraph to *One Life*.

p. 98. (a) Thoreau confessed to slaying trees in *Walden*, p. 27.

(b) The well-known quote about wildness comes from an 1862 essay by Thoreau entitled "Walking." It is the motto of the Wilderness Society, and the title and epitaph of a collection of Eliot Porter photographs [Eliot Porter, *In Wildness is the Preservation of the World* (San Francisco: Sierra Club Books, 1962)].

p. 99. (a) The hilltop clearcut is mentioned in *Walden*, p. 58.

(b) Thoreau's description of the Fitchburg Railway is found on p. 27 of *Walden*.

p. 101. (a) Ellery Channing's tease was quoted by Joseph Wood Krutch in his essay "Paradise Found," reprinted in *Walden*, pp. 327-35: the Channing material appears on p. 330.

(b) Thoreau's musings on pumpkins and shiftlessness are found in *Walden*, p. 44.

p. 102. (a) The quote about the doormat comes from *Walden*, p. 45.

(b) The passage about the three pieces of limestone is from *Walden*, p. 24.

(c) Thoreau's reasons for leaving the woods are discussed on p. 213 of *Walden*.

p. 111. (a) The various anti-environmentalist quotes on this page come from no specific source: they are merely representative of the types of slurs that were being heard commonly in Oregon during the period of the spotted owl hearings.

(b) The Board of Commissioners' statement about "critical levels of confusion . . ." may be found in Monica Alleven, "It's owls vs. timber," *Ashland (Oregon) Daily Tidings*, May 4, 1989, p. 1.

p. 118: The quotes from Gary Schrodt on this page are from Alleven, *ibid*.

p. 128-29: Bernstein found Hershberger Mountain "magical" in Art Bernstein, *76 Day Hikes Within 100 Miles of the Rogue Valley* (Grants Pass, Oregon: New Leaf Books, 1987), p. 83.

p. 132. The advice from the King of Hearts to the White Rabbit (often erroneously attributed to the rabbit himself) comes from Lewis Carroll, *Alice in Wonderland*, chapter 12. In the edition I have at hand (New York: Lancer Books Magnum Easy Eye Edition, 1968) it is found on p. 133.

p. 136. My somewhat purple description of Valley of the Drums was published in William Ashworth, *Nor Any Drop To Drink* (New York: Summit Books, 1982), p. 165.

p. 144. (a) Muir's journal entry regarding the Crater Lake rain may be found in Linnie Marsh Wolfe, ed., *John of the Mountains: The Unpublished Journals of John Muir* (Madison, Wisconsin: University of Wisconsin Press, 1979, hereinafter cited as Wolfe), p. 357.

(b) Pinchot's description of Muir's conversational prowess comes from *Breaking New Ground*, p. 101.

p. 145. (a) Pinchot's description of the Sierra comes from *Breaking New Ground*, p. 103.

(b) The participants' separate accounts of that night on the rim of the Grand Canyon—including all the quotes reproduced here—can be found in *Breaking New Ground*, p. 103, and Wolfe, p. 363.

p. 146. The "guilty schoolboys" passage comes from *Breaking New Ground*, p. 103.

p. 163. There are many sources for "Cock Robin," which appears to date back to at least the 14th century: see, e.g., Alan Lomax, *The Folk Songs of North America* (New York: Doubleday, 1960), p. 181. It appears here as I usually perform it.

p. 169. (a) The quote about lands "instinct with God" appears in Muir's journal entry for September 4, 1908 (quoted here from Wolfe, p. 437).

(b) The bit about "horizontal brothers" is found in Wolfe, p. 277, where it is part of a rough journal sketch which later became Muir's well-known dog story "Stickeen."

p. 174. (a) Aldo Leopold on conservation comes from the foreword to *A Sand County Almanac*. In my edition (New York: Ballantine Books, 1970) it is found on pp. xviii-xix.

(b) The Thoreau quote about wildness has been previously cited (notes to p. 98); the Pinchot quote comes from *Breaking New Ground*, p. 104.

p. 175. Actually, James Hilton did not write "Moderation in all things, including moderation." Although this idea is commonly accepted as the central message of *Lost Horizon*, its only explicit expression in the book is couched in somewhat different language: " . . . our prevalent belief is in moderation. We inculcate the virtue of avoiding excess of all kind—even including, if you will pardon the paradox, excess of virtue itself." (James Hilton, *Lost Horizon* [New York: Pocket Books, 1939], p. 58.)

p. 177. The legend of "Desiderata" having been found in a 17th-century church has taken on a life of its own, but the piece was actually written in 1927 by Max Ehrmann. See, e.g., Fred D. Cavinder, "Desiderata," *TWA Ambassador*, Aug. 1973, pp. 14-15.

p. 185. The Stan Rogers quote I have paraphrased here can be found in the liner notes to his album *From Fresh Water* (Hamilton, Ontario, Canada: Cole Harbour, 1984). Stan was actually paraphrasing, also—from Robert Heinlein—but no matter.